Acknowledgements

We would like to thank all the people who contributed to the writing of this book: the anonymous readers for their feedback, the various teachers on courses who inspired us, the teachers who helped test the assessment tasks, and the children we taught, whom this book is for.

We'd also like to thank Ann Hunter and say a big thank you to Julia Sallabank who was so patient with us and for all the valuable constructive feedback she offered us, and Alan Maley and Cristina Whitecross for believing in the need for a book on assessment for young learners.

Sophie Ioannou-Georgiou would also like to thank Michael Matsangos and Andreas Loizides for their support throughout her service at Cyprus primaries, Yiannakis and Dina Ioannou for their unconditional love, Stephanie Constantia and Melina for putting up with an absent-minded and busy mum, and Yiannis for his invaluable support and patience.

Pavlos Pavlou would like to take this opportunity to express his gratitude to his teachers, Paul Angelis and Lise Winer, for their inspiring role and constant encouragement in his studies and teaching career. Also he wishes to thank his mother Anastasia, wife Crissa, and adorable son Yiangos for their love and support.

The authors and publisher are grateful to those who have given permission to reproduce the following extracts and adaptations of copyright material:

p.88 Extract from *Pat and Her Picture* by Rosemary Border © Oxford University Press 1988. Reproduced by permission.

p.88 Extract from *April Fool's Day* by L. G. Alexander reproduced by permission of Julia Alexander.

p.158 Information about Edinburgh Zoo. Reproduced by permission.

Although every effort has been made to trace and contact copyright holders before publication, this has not been possible in some cases. We apologize for any apparent infringement of copyright and, if notified, the publisher will be pleased to rectify any errors or omissions at the earliest opportunity.

Illustrations by Margaret Welbank © Oxford University Press.

Contents

The authors and series editor

Sophie Ioannou-Georgiou trained as a primary school teacher and then went on to specialize in the teaching of English as a Foreign Language. She studied for a Postgraduate Diploma in TEFL and then for an MA in TEFL at the University of Reading. She has taught EFL at a variety of levels and institutions and has also worked for the Cyprus Ministry of Education and Culture as part of a team to produce a series of textbooks for the teaching of EFL at Cyprus State Primary Schools. Until recently she worked as a teacher trainer and dealt with the in-service training of primary school teachers at the Cyprus Pedagogical Institute. She is currently studying for a PhD at the University of Nottingham.

Pavlos Pavlou is an applied linguist, teacher trainer, and language teacher. He received his education at the University of Vienna, Austria, Southern Illinois University Carbondale, USA (MA in Applied Linguistics and German) and at Georgetown University (PhD in Applied Linguistics). He has taught linguistics, English for Academic Purposes, and English, French, German, and Greek as a Foreign Language at all levels at various colleges and language schools in Cyprus. Since 1997 he has been working at the Department of Foreign Languages and Literatures at the University of Cyprus where he teaches EFL methodology, language testing, and sociolinguistics. He also participates in the pre-service training for English teachers organized by the Cyprus Pedagogical Institute.

Alan Maley worked for The British Council from 1962 to 1988, serving as English Language Officer in Yugoslavia, Ghana, Italy, France, and China, and as Regional Representative in South India (Madras). From 1988 to 1993 he was Director-General of the Bell Educational Trust, Cambridge. From 1993 to 1998 he was Senior Fellow in the Department of English Language and Literature of the National University of Singapore. He is currently a freelance consultant and Director of the graduate programme at Assumption University, Bangkok. Among his publications are *Literature*, in this series, *Beyond Words*, *Sounds Interesting*, *Sounds Intriguing*, *Words*, *Variations on a Theme*, and *Drama Techniques in Language Learning* (all with Alan Duff), *The Mind's Eye* (with Françoise Grellet and Alan Duff), *Learning to Listen* and *Poem into Poem* (with Sandra Moulding), *Short and Sweet*, and *The English Teacher's Voice*.

Foreword

It is generally accepted that we teach young learners differently from older ones. A whole range of entertaining, motivating, creative, and above all, physically engaging activities has been developed in recent years, to keep pace with the growth in demand for materials to teach this special group of learners. However, when it comes to assessing the progress of young learners, we often find ourselves driven back on testing materials which are more appropriate for use with older learners.

This book will therefore be particularly welcome as it attempts to link assessment with instruction. If teaching is focused on physically engaging, creative, entertaining activities, then these should also be the focus of any assessment which is carried out. Teaching and assessment thus become congruent, not inconsistent.

The book advocates the active involvement of children in their own assessment. A number of suggestions are made for doing this. These include the use of language portfolios, which constitute a running record of the child's progress in consultation with the child; structured assessment activities/tasks, where 'normal' activities are given an assessment focus; projects; self-assessment; peer assessment; learner-developed assessment tasks; and observation/conferencing. There is even a place for more traditional tests in this scheme. It is important to emphasize this wide range of assessment tools, since it gives the teacher flexibility to take account of learner/group differences, and the ability to decide on more or less formal/consultative modes of assessment to suit each case.

It should be stressed that, although the forms of assessment closely mirror the forms of teaching, they have a clearly defined, distinct focus. The aims, criteria, and measurable results mark assessment off from 'normal' teaching activities. This book therefore satisfies the justifiable desire on the part of parents, schools, and other authorities for evidence that learning has taken place. But, above all, it can contribute to the children's sense of pride in their achievement, and thus motivate them to make further progress.

Alan Maley

Introduction

This book proposes ways of assessing children learning English as a second or foreign language and provides ideas for classroom-based assessment. Although some of the assessment activities may also be relevant to external exams such as the UCLES Young Learners Exams, the main concern of this book is to provide assessment closely related to the learning process. By this we mean that the purpose of the assessment ideas outlined here is to serve teaching and learning by providing feedback to you and the children, encouraging a positive classroom atmosphere, and promoting and maintaining strong motivation for learning English.

Who is this book for?

Young learners

The assessment tasks and techniques in this book are aimed at primary and early secondary school children aged six to twelve learning English as a second or foreign language. Children in this age group can sometimes be negatively affected by assessment techniques used for older learners. What this book suggests is an approach more suited to the needs of 6–12 year olds.

Children vary in maturity, learning experiences, and overall background. Consequently, the techniques we recommend may be suitable for the target age group in one context, but not for the same age group in another context. Your role as the teacher is very important, since only you can judge whether a technique is suitable for your class or not. An assessment activity pitched at the children's level may be very motivating for them, whereas one designed for a different level can be quite damaging. Most of the assessment techniques in this book suggest a number of possible variations, enabling you to choose the variation best suited to your class.

Teachers

This book will be useful to both experienced teachers and new teachers who:

- teach young children and want help on how to assess them
- do not want the curriculum to be dictated by the syllabus of external exams
- want to have a say in how their children are assessed
- want child-friendly, classroom-based assessment

- question whether traditional assessment methods are suitable for their pupils and want to try alternative methods of assessment
- are studying assessment methods at college, university, or teacher training college.

It is also for teacher-trainers who want to recommend appropriate assessment approaches for use with children.

Evaluation, assessment, and testing

The terms evaluation, assessment, and testing are often confused and used interchangeably. They do not, however, mean the same thing. Testing is just one part of assessment. Assessment and evaluation are more general, more global processes.

Evaluation

Evaluation is the process of gathering information in order to determine the extent to which a language programme meets its goals. Relevant information can be teachers' and parents' opinions, textbook quality, exam results, and children's attitudes. Some of the tools of the evaluation process are tests, questionnaires, textbook analysis, and observation.

Assessment

This is a general term which includes all methods used to gather information about children's knowledge, ability, understanding, attitudes, and motivation. Assessment can be carried out through a number of instruments (for example, tests, self-assessment), and can be formal or informal.

Testing

Testing is one of the procedures that can be used to assess a child's performance. A test has a certain objective, for example, to see to what extent a child understands a written text. The test then checks whether the child has achieved this objective. Testing uses tasks or exercises and assigns marks or grades based on quantifiable results.

Teaching and assessment

As a teacher, you are accountable for children's progress first to the children themselves, also to the parents, the head teacher, the school authorities, and others. Consequently, you need evidence of the children's progress. Resorting to traditional tests, although they are widely accepted and generally considered objective, is not the ideal solution for children. Children are different from other groups of learners. Traditional tests can have negative effects on their self-esteem, motivation, and overall attitudes towards learning and the target language.

The recognition that children have special needs has led to the development of effective teaching methodologies that take into account children's creativity and their love of play, songs, rhymes, activity, and role play. These methodologies also recognize children's limitations in terms of their short attention span, their cognitive development, and their specific areas of interest. As these methodologies have been introduced into classroom teaching, classrooms have become more learner-centred and child-friendly.

Assessment, on the other hand, although an integral part of teaching that should reflect and complement the methodologies used in class, has not developed in the same way. This problem has long been recognized but only recently addressed. Some teachers resort to external exams under pressure of accountability, tailoring their lessons to train their children for the chosen exam. In so doing, they often miss out on methodologies appropriate to children.

This book responds to the need to assess children appropriately. The assessment tools we advocate are based on communicative language learning, task-based learning, appropriateness for children, authenticity, learner training, learner autonomy, and critical reflection. The assessment tasks we suggest are closely linked to the classroom practices used today with children. The children will therefore be familiar with the format of the assessment tasks, so they don't see them as something different or alien, and the tasks do not create anxiety or other negative feelings. On the contrary, they can encourage positive attitudes in that they may be seen as a fun thing to do.

Why assess young children?

Assessment may at first sound threatening and not suited to a child's nature, but it is a necessary part of teaching and learning. Assessment can serve the following purposes:

To monitor and aid children's progress

A teacher needs to be constantly aware of what the children know, what difficulties they are experiencing, and how best to help them. On the basis of assessment outcomes you are able to give individualized help to each child.

To provide children with evidence of their progress and enhance motivation

Assessment results give children tangible evidence of their progress. Learning a language is a long process. Achieving short-term goals (for example, knowing the colours, being able to tell the time) can boost children's motivation and encourage them to persist in their efforts.

Assessment can also help children to focus on areas that need more work before they can achieve a short-term goal. Becoming aware of the progress expected of them within a given time-frame can motivate children, as they see themselves getting closer to their goal. This makes them try harder to achieve their goal. When they have positive assessment results before them, they feel their efforts are worthwhile. This encourages them to keep on trying. This is why it is so important to pitch assessment activities to the children's level. To encourage weaker children, it may sometimes even be a good idea to give them an easier test.

To monitor your performance and plan future work

The information you get from assessment can help you to evaluate your own work, to find out how effective you have been and how successful your chosen methodology or materials were. You are then able to plan, modifying aspects of your teaching (books, materials, methodology, etc.) as necessary, and develop techniques and methods for responding to the children's individual needs.

To provide information for parents, colleagues, and school authorities

Many other people, besides the children and the teacher, need to be kept informed on the children's progress. Parents, for example, need to know whether their children's efforts and the school's/teacher's language programme are yielding satisfactory results. Colleagues benefit when assessment results are kept by the school and passed on to future class teachers. This gives them a profile of each child's strengths and weaknesses. Moreover, the teachers themselves know that they will often be judged by the school on the basis of the learners' results among other things. Assessment results are then seen as evidence of the teacher's teaching effectiveness.

What do we assess?

The following skills and attitudes should be assessed:

Skills development

Although language often involves the use of all four skills in an integrated way, in assessment we may want to consider each skill separately, so that we can examine the children's progress and/or detect problems in that particular skill. This can sometimes be difficult because assessing one skill often requires the use of another. In such cases you need to ensure that your main focus is on the skill you are assessing.

Listening is an active skill that includes the use of many sub-skills such as predicting content, inferring meaning from content, listening for gist, and listening for detailed information. Children are able to use the basic sub-skills in their own language. Some of these sub-skills, such as inferring meaning and predicting content, should also be practised in the foreign language class. Training children to do this gives them a head start in their learning career. Assessment should, therefore, check progress in a variety of listening sub-skills.

Speaking also consists of a number of elements such as pronunciation, intonation, and turn-taking. But the overall aim of speaking is to achieve oral communication, i.e. to be able to convey messages. When assessing children, the emphasis should be on their communicative ability in basic functions such as asking questions or introducing themselves.

Reading involves various sub-skills similar to the ones in listening: reading for detail (intensive reading), reading for gist (skimming), reading for specific information (scanning), predicting content, and inferring meaning from content and context. Again it is important to help children to develop these sub-skills. They are helpful as learning strategies which will, in turn, make for successful reading and thus increase children's exposure to the target language. Therefore reading sub-skills should be regularly assessed.

Writing is considered the most difficult language skill, since it includes so many other elements such as handwriting, spelling, syntax, grammar, paragraphing, ideas, etc. For this age group the most important writing skills are mastering the Roman alphabet, copying, handwriting, spelling, and basic sentence formation.

Integrated skills Assessing skills separately may be justified for assessment purposes but often it does not reflect real-life language use. All language skills are integrated in real life and rarely used in isolation. For this reason, they should also be assessed integratively. Assessing integrated skills allows for techniques that simulate real-life situations and monitor the children's ability to cope in situations where they have to draw on more than one language skill.

Learning how to learn

In today's fast-changing world, children have to be trained to use a variety of learning skills and to discover the most effective ones for them. This will help them to become autonomous learners and to deal with the constant need to acquire new knowledge.

Skills such as using a dictionary, the Internet or other resources, checking and reflecting on their own learning, reviewing their work, and organizing their learning will maximize the results of the children's efforts. They should, therefore, also be assessed in these skills. Assessing learning-how-to-learn skills is important since it will help children realize the importance of such skills, and also help them to develop useful learning habits and influence the rest of their learning career.

Attitudes

Fostering positive attitudes in childhood should be a priority, since this is the best time to form strong positive attitudes towards learning, the target language, and the target culture. Negative attitudes formed at this stage are hard to change in the future.

Attitude assessment can be done during conferencing (short, private conversations with the children) or through questionnaires and observation. Although it is not possible to award objective marks for attitudes, motivation, pleasure in learning, and interest in the target culture, you can create profiles of individual children, describing their attitudes, and compile reports for parents, colleagues, and school authorities. Most importantly, assessment of attitudes will enable you to intervene if a child expresses over-negative feelings.

Behavioural and social skills

Teachers, regardless of their individual subjects, are above all charged with the education and development of the child as a whole person. Becoming a good team member, being polite, being sensitive to others' feelings and appreciative of their efforts are some of the qualities all subject teachers should promote and assess.

How do we assess children?

Children usually do not choose to learn a foreign language. The decision is made for them either by their parents or by the school authorities. They are still too young to recognize the usefulness of a foreign language. Therefore they need other reasons to motivate them and to keep them learning. A friendly environment can offer such motivations. You can make learning as enjoyable as possible through drawing, games, songs, puzzles, and drama.

Nevertheless, your hard work in establishing a motivating atmosphere and positive attitudes towards learning English can be severely damaged when it comes time for assessment. To avoid this, we propose that you carry out assessment in a way that protects the positive atmosphere and attitudes towards English and learning in general. Some of the methods we propose are: structured assessment activities/tasks, take-home assessment tasks, portfolio assessment, and other methods discussed below. We believe these methods not only preserve but also enhance the positive learning atmosphere in a classroom.

In presenting the assessment methods which follow, we have discussed each one separately for reasons of clarity and practicality. They are, however, interrelated. The use of portfolios as an assessment tool is a method that includes all the others. A portfolio creates a complete picture of a child's achievement by collating information obtained through tests, projects, and conferencing notes. Projects, on the other hand, can involve structured assessment tasks, self- and peer-assessment, as well as observation notes. Classroom assessment that generates useful information for teaching and learning will naturally involve the use of more than one of the following methods of assessment.

Portfolio assessment

A language portfolio is a collection of samples of work produced by the child over a period of time. These samples can include written work, drawings, projects, a record of books read, recordings (audio or video), test results, self-assessment records, and teacher and parent comments. The children are ultimately responsible for their portfolio. The choice of what goes into the portfolios is based on specific criteria agreed on by you and the children together.

Keeping a portfolio is an ongoing process which includes selection of work samples, portfolio review, withdrawal of samples, deciding on new additions, etc. A portfolio is useful to you when you are carrying out your assessment or profiling, because it offers you a more complete picture of a child's work and development than any other assessment technique. It is also important to parents, future teachers, and school authorities because it gives them a complete picture of what the child is able to do and enables them to see the child's progress over the year. Primarily, however, the portfolio should be for the children themselves. This is especially true of young learners, for whom the portfolio can be an exciting project and the showcase for their new-found knowledge and ability.

Structured assessment activities/tasks

Structured assessment activities are tasks organized by the teacher in order to assess knowledge, skills (including communication skills), and attitudes, as well as the ability to apply these to new situations.

These activities/tasks can be constructed in such a way that they reflect sound teaching principles such as creating authentic, child-centred activities. Activities particularly suitable for children are ones in which they demonstrate understanding by doing. Activities such as drawing, miming, cutting and pasting, pointing, touching, etc. are particularly useful for assessing receptive skills, since they do not require verbal performance.

Drawing activities, for example, allow children to respond to a question or solve a task, thus demonstrating their understanding and awareness of the language without having to use verbal communication. For younger or shy children who may need a silent period before starting to use the language and for weaker children who may be lacking in productive skills, this can be an effective way of allowing them to demonstrate their abilities.

Projects

Projects are especially suitable for assessing mixed-ability groups. You can assign or avoid assigning specific tasks according to the children's particular abilities. Moreover, projects lend themselves to integrating language skills and promoting student creativity. Projects can, however, be more demanding in terms of organization and assessment because they involve assessing both group work and individual contribution to the group. For advice and ideas, see *Projects with Young Learners* in this series.

Self-assessment

Self-assessment is extremely important in that it promotes invaluable learning skills such as monitoring one's own progress, reflecting on one's abilities and learning styles, and setting personal goals. It also gives children an insight into the assessment criteria used by others. Furthermore, the children benefit from feeling that they have a say in their assessment. This gives them a certain sense of empowerment.

Children are able to use basic criteria to assess themselves but they may need more guidance and time than older learners. Expect children to take a long time before they are able to use self-assessment effectively – be patient and persistent! It is important that you recognize the amount of time and guidance the children will need before becoming familiar with each task type.

Some of the most widely used self-assessment methods are: portfolios, questionnaires, conferencing, graphic representations, and dialogue journals. They can all be used with children, even if the process has to be carried out initially in the mother tongue.

Peer-assessment

Learning and assessment can be more fun when it is done with friends. Peer-assessment can positively influence the classroom atmosphere because children learn to respect and accept each other through assessing each other's work. Peer-assessment fosters the feeling that the classroom is a community working towards the same goal. Over time, this sense of community carries over into other classroom activities as well. It minimizes the negative aspects of competition and encourages trust among children. The children also discover that they can learn from their peers, not just from their teacher, and gain further insight and responsibility in applying assessment criteria.

As is the case with self-assessment, children may take some time before they can carry out peer-assessment effectively. Some children may continue to be self-centred and immature, but repeated practice of peer-assessment, objective assessment criteria, and the presence of a teacher who is fair and appreciative of the children's efforts, will eventually lead to the resolution of most personality/maturity problems.

Traditional tests

There are certain advantages to using traditional tests such as multiple-choice questions, true-false statements, and cloze-tests. They are objective, easy to mark, and easy to prepare. Nevertheless, the traditional testing philosophy is not an ideal approach for children. Children see tests as intimidating and stressful. Furthermore, we should bear in mind that traditional tests do not tell us much about what children can actually do. All they usually give the children as feedback is a grade or mark. Any information on children's progress derived from traditional tests should usually be complemented with information gathered through other assessment techniques.

Learner-developed assessment tasks

Children can contribute to the content of an assessment task or actually create a task of their own. Discussion of task content with the teacher helps to encourage responsibility and maturity, because the children have to think about what they are supposed to know and have to set appropriate performance criteria.

When children are involved in preparing the assessment task or parts of the task themselves, the assessment procedure becomes even more personalized and less threatening. The children may make materials to be included in the task, write questions from which you select a sample, write questions for others to answer, or write sentences or paragraphs to be used as reading comprehension assessment tasks.

Take-home tasks

A take-home task is one that children can complete at home after discussion with you. The children are given a deadline to meet. Such tasks are usually integrative (e.g. projects) and have a number of advantages. They are particularly suitable for mixed-ability classes, because the children have the freedom to choose how to go about completing their task, how much time to spend on it, when to work on it, and what level of performance they perceive as satisfactory in the light of their own abilities.

Take-home assessment tasks also foster autonomous learning, since the children assume responsibility for completing the task on their own, disciplining themselves, setting their own deadlines, deciding how much time they need to complete the task, and ensuring the completion, quality, and return of the task to the teacher. All of these steps go hand-in-hand with learning-how-to-learn skills.

Observation

You observe your children every single lesson and make dozens of judgements every day. Are the children following the instructions? Is Costas performing the task correctly? Is José bored? All these considerations are a continuous assessment of the children's behaviour, attitudes, and performance. However, these observations are not usually systematically recorded and so cannot be used for assessment purposes.

To record observations systematically, try to make short notes soon after the lesson and, keep them on file; or you can use checklists (see 10.8), and tick them during or after the lesson. Even organized in this way, observations are very subjective and should be used in combination with other assessment methods.

Conferencing

By conferencing we mean informal and friendly chats you have with the children, during which they should feel comfortable enough to express themselves freely. Conferencing may be carried out either on a one-to-one basis or in small groups of four or five children. In rare cases you may have the luxury of being able to take the children to another room for conferencing. More often, your only option is to do your conferencing while the rest of the class is engaged in written or other work.

Conferencing can take place at the beginning of the course, when a new child joins the class, at the end of a specific unit, during portfolio reviews, before an important exam, or when there is a specific problem to deal with.

You can also use conferencing to assess speaking skills, in which case you do it in the target language and use appropriate activities. It is particularly suitable for assessing attitudes, learning styles, and extensive reading. You can also use it in portfolio assessment and to complete or check information you have gathered through observation or other methods. If you are using conferencing as a means of assessing attitudes or skills other than speaking, we recommend you do it in the children's mother tongue when the children's ability in English is limited.

It might be helpful to give children some questions to think about beforehand, e.g. *What do you think is your best piece of work?*

If finding time for conferences is very difficult, you could perhaps consider a written conference where children fill in an evaluation sheet or questionnaire and you comment on it.

Is this assessment?

If you have been using traditional tests, you may understandably be questioning the suitability of the proposed tasks as assessment tools. Understandably, because the tasks represent a different approach to assessment and probably look much more like classroom activities. However, it is our firm belief that assessment tasks for classroom-based assessment should reflect teaching practices. Despite their resemblance to classroom activities, the proposed assessment methods are different from teaching activities in the following ways:

Aims Assessment tasks aim to check children's language-learning progress. You do them in order to assess the children's progress, not to teach or practise language. The assessment tasks are therefore constructed in such a way that the area to be assessed is clearly defined and isolated from other areas. If, for example, our aim is to assess reading, children will not be required to write; if our aim is to assess listening, the children will not be asked to produce spoken or written language.

Measurable results Assessment tasks produce measurable evidence of each individual child's language development. After you have carried out an assessment task you will know exactly what each child can or cannot do in terms of the predetermined aims of the activity. (For example, you will know that *Evi can say the colours. Nacia can recognize the numbers 1–10.*)

Assessment criteria Each assessment task specifies a set of criteria defining what the children should be able to do in order to demonstrate their grasp of the particular area assessed. The assessment criteria are expressed as actions through which the children demonstrate their ability/development.

Children's predisposition towards the activity When older children know they are going to be assessed, they will usually prepare beforehand, do their best during the assessment, and take more notice of post-assessment feedback. These behaviours are noticeably different from the children's usual behaviour in the classroom.

Timing Assessment tasks are set at specific times during the learning process, usually at the end of a unit, or after presentation and practice of specific language items or skills, so that you can check the children's learning. They can also be used diagnostically when you want to find out what the children already know.

Children's participation Children have to take part in assessment tasks, whereas you may allow children not to participate in regular class activities or accept the fact that some children are not very active contributors. Many classroom activities give you an overview of the performance and abilities of the class as a whole and possibly detailed insight into the performance and ability of a small number of children. An assessment task, however, should give you information on the performance and ability of every child in the class.

Record keeping/learner profiling Children's performance in an assessment task is recorded and kept on file. Additions or notes relevant to the children's performance in the assessment task can also be used when writing their profile. This helps you to be organized and well informed about each individual child, and allows you to report back to all the interested parties fully and confidently.

How to give feedback

Assessment is not complete as soon as you collect the children's work. Offering feedback is an integral part of the assessment process and should follow as soon as possible after the assessment task is carried out. The longer we delay giving feedback, the less meaningful it becomes and the less impact it has on the children.

Feedback can be given in a variety of ways: individually to each child, to groups of children, or to the whole class. It can also be given in the form of self-correction or peer-feedback. Feedback helps children to discover their strengths and weaknesses, motivates them, and helps them to persist in their learning. A number or a letter grade cannot do this for weaker children, the ones most in need of encouragement and motivation.

One of the best ways to give feedback is through conferencing with the children, when you discuss the results of the assessment. If face-to-face conferencing is not possible, then you can respond to the children's journal entries. Or you can give written feedback in the form of short comments, and follow it up with a brief chat.

Peer-feedback can be important to children because it comes from their friends. Train the children to appreciate peer-feedback and to give feedback constructively. If there is a friendly and supportive atmosphere in class, the whole class can sometimes offer feedback to one child. It is important in these circumstances that all the children agree and take turns to have their work discussed by the others.

Marking schemes

Marking schemes are a way of indicating the level to which a learner has achieved the aims of the assessment task. This book uses the following marking schemes:

– discrete-point marking schemes
– speaking marking schemes
– writing marking schemes.

Discrete-point marking schemes

This type of marking scheme is used for activities that have clear-cut, objective answers. You can allocate a specific number of points to each assessment item and, depending on the number of items, you can decide whether to allocate marks out of 100, 20, 10, etc. When you allocate points, decide what you consider important and what you are trying to assess. If, for example, you are assessing reading comprehension, you should not give marks for grammatical accuracy. Rather, you should reward responses that indicate comprehension. If you are assessing writing and you think that clear handwriting is also important, you can award points for clear handwriting.

The way you allocate points indicates what you think is important for the children's development and success in language learning. Share this with the children. It is not only fair, but good practice, to tell the children how they will be assessed and how you allocate points. This information helps the children to prepare for the task more effectively. Insight into your assessment criteria will also help to guide them towards developing their own criteria on what is important for successful language learning.

Discrete-point marking schemes are usually associated with a number or a mark. Although marking or grading an assessment task with a number may be easy and fast, it does not give you, the children, or the parents any real information. What have the children been assessed in? What can they do now? If you are going to use marks, it is better if the number or mark is accompanied by a comment (usually in the mother tongue) addressing the individual performance of each child. There is an example on the next page.

If children cannot read at all (not even in their mother tongue), consider commenting on their work during short one-to-one conversations.

Speaking and writing marking schemes

The speaking and writing assessment tasks in this book use the marking schemes for speaking and writing outlined in Chapter 10, 'Record keeping and reporting'. The format serves two purposes:

– It is more practical and less time-consuming to fill in a report at the same time as you are actually marking the outcome of an assessment activity.
– It helps you to make sure you use the same criteria you applied during assessment when reporting children's progress.

1 Assessing recognition of animal names (reading):

9–10	Very good.	You can read the names of all the animals we learnt.
6–8	Good.	You can read the names of animals well!
3–5	Good but you could do even better.	You can read the names of some of the animals. What about the rest?
0–2	Try harder! You can do it!	You can try harder to learn to read the names of the animals. Would you like that? Can I help you?

2 Assessing copying skills (writing mechanics):

9–10	Very good.	You can copy words very well!
6–8	Good.	You can copy words well!
3–5	Good but you could do even better.	You copied most of the words well! Did you need more time?
0–2	Try harder! You can do it!	Good try! Be careful to spot the differences between the letters **h** and **n**, **g** and **q**.

Assessment of group work

Children usually enjoy working and learning in groups, and group assessment may feel much safer than individual exposure. Group assessment is also suitable for mixed-ability classes, because it allows children to help and be helped by their peers. In that respect group work also provides opportunities for assessment of valuable social skills such as co-operation.

Nonetheless, group work poses challenges for assessment. How do you assess the group as a whole without ignoring the contribution of the individual? How do you balance the work of the individual against that of the group? It is important to assess the group as a whole, otherwise why assign and assess group work anyway? On the other hand you cannot ignore the work of the child who may or may not have contributed to the group in an adequate manner.

Our suggestion is to assess both the group and the individual and to document your assessment on a single report, so as to emphasize the value of both. The sample report on page 18 provides the means of assessing the group as a whole on issues such as completion of the task, use of the target language, and co-operative behaviour. You can also assess and report on how successfully the task was completed. This is reflected in the categories 'Completed the task successfully' and 'Carried out his/her task successfully'.

Although this may seem like just another general category, the achievement itself changes each time because it refers to the different aims of different tasks. If, for example, the task is an oral presentation, a role play, or the creation of a poster, the different objectives of each task will be reflected in this category. To clarify this, you may add to your file or staple on to each child's report the name of the task and its particular aim.

The section on the individual child's work begins with identifying what his/her individual responsibilities and contributions were. Once you have recorded the child's responsibilities, you can assess how well they were carried out, and you can assess the child's performance in terms of use of the target language, contribution to the group, and co-operation.

To fill in the form, put a mark on the line between 'Yes' and 'No' to show how well you think this aspect has been carried out. For example:

helped the group   Yes _____/_____ No

Assessment of group work can also take the form of self- or peer-assessment. If you decide to use these forms of assessment, again you could use the sample report. In the case of peer-assessment the gaps are filled in the same way. If you choose to use it for self-assessment, you would need to make minor changes such as 'My group', 'My contribution', 'I carried out my task successfully', etc.

Finally, you may decide to choose a combination of peer-, teacher-, and self-assessment, using the first part as teacher-assessment and the second part as self-assessment, etc.

A final word

We hope that you will find this book useful and that it will help you in your efforts to assess children in an effective, fruitful, and enjoyable way. We are sure that the tasks you find in this book will stimulate in you similar ideas on assessing young learners. We wish you and your children every success in this important and exciting venture!

Group work assessment form

Name _____   Task _____

Group _____   Date _____

_____'s group:

completed the task on time	Yes _____	No
worked well together	Yes _____	No
completed the task successfully	Yes _____	No
used English a lot	Yes _____	No

Comments

_____'s contribution to the group

The group asked _____ to:

1 _____

2 _____

  _____

helped the group	Yes _____	No
used English a lot	Yes _____	No
worked well with the other children	Yes _____	No
carried out his/her task successfully	Yes _____	No

Comments

How to use this book

This book offers a variety of assessment tasks suitable for use with young learners. It provides a wealth of examples for assessing language learning at different levels. It cannot, however, cover every case you may need to assess. Each class and each child is different. You may sometimes need to use one of the variations suggested or adapt the tasks to your children's needs.

Nevertheless, we believe that this book can give you a head start in using appropriate and child-friendly approaches to assessment and help you to use them in such a way that you ultimately develop your own assessment tasks closely adapted to your situation.

How the book is organized

The book contains ten chapters: Chapter 1 presents the basics of portfolio assessment relevant to all the chapters that follow. Chapters 2–5 are devoted to the four language skills, Chapter 6 focuses on assessing integrated skills through projects, Chapters 7–9 cover grammar, self-assessment, and learning-how-to-learn skills, and Chapter 10 focuses on recording and reporting progress.

How each assessment task is organized

The assessment tasks are organized according to the following categories:

Level

The levels given should be regarded as a rough guide, since children vary in maturity, background, and other factors. Other factors can also influence their language learning. Courses in different countries vary in level, length, and intensity. We recommend that when you plan to use a specific assessment task, you decide whether it is suitable for your children's level or not. You are the ultimate judge.

Beginners Children at this level can be divided into three sub-groups:

Complete beginners: Children with no knowledge of English.

False beginners: Children with some knowledge of English, not necessarily from lessons. A child at this level may also be familiar with common expressions such as *Hello! Thank you*, etc.

Advanced beginners: Children who have been taught English at school or in private classes for a year (or have had the equivalent of 80–100 hours of instruction). Children in this category can be expected to know: colours, numbers, days of the week, animals, food items, school objects, furniture, the verb *to be*, *I've got/I haven't got*, *I can/can't*, *I like/I don't like*, etc.

Elementary   Children at this level may have had between two and three years of English (or the equivalent of 100–300 hours of instruction). In addition to what they should know from beginner level, they should theoretically be able to talk about themselves, their family, daily routines, tell the time, describe people, pets, and their house or room.

Pre-intermediate   Children at this level would normally have had three to five years of English (or the equivalent of 240–500 hours of instruction) and are probably confident and familiar with everything at elementary level. In addition they should be able to give longer descriptions of things, people, and places, longer accounts of events, using the present simple and possibly the present continuous and past simple.

Age group

In the assessment tasks the age groups have been divided into:
• 6 and above
• 8 and above
• 10 and above

Time

This is an indication of how long the assessment task will take. It does not include time for preparation, feedback, or follow-up. Class size and other factors such as the children's familiarity with the task format and co-operation on the part of the children may have an effect on the time needed for each assessment task.

Description

This is a brief summary of the assessment task to give you an overview of what it involves.

Language

This is the language needed to carry out the task you are going to assess.

Skills

The aim of each assessment task is expressed in terms of a skill/sub-skill.

Assessment criteria

These are the performance standards by which we judge whether the children have achieved the aims of an assessment task. They are expressed in terms of behaviour.

Materials

This includes everything you need to prepare for the task.

Preparation

This indicates what you need to do before carrying out the assessment task.

In class

This is a step-by-step guide to carrying out the assessment task.

Feedback

After an assessment task, time should be allotted to feedback. This is the time when the children reflect on how they have performed. At this stage children may also express their feelings about the assessment task.

Follow-up

The aim, topic, or product of the assessment task can provide an impetus for other learning activities. Under this heading, we offer ideas on how you can exploit an assessment task for further learning.

Variations

Depending on your particular context or set of circumstances (you have a large class, for example, or no access to a photocopier or overhead projector) you may need to make changes to the assessment tasks. The Variations present some suggestions along these lines.

Assessment of outcome

In assessment, you need to have certain criteria against which you can measure the successful completion of a task. This is done by looking at the product/outcome of the activity. It can be done by you (teacher-assessment), the children themselves (self-assessment), or other children (peer-assessment). It can also be done in a variety of ways depending on the task, the age, and the level of the children (journal writing, conferencing, for example). Assessment of outcome often includes portfolio assessment which is, however, presented in a separate category.

Portfolio

This gives ideas on how to use the portfolio with the assessment task, and usually gives ideas for making assessment results more meaningful, say, by including the child's or your comments, or by adding other forms of assessment like journal writing, observation notes, or parents' comments to supplement the assessment task results. See Chapter 1 for more on portfolios.

Comments

The comments provide information that does not fit under other categories.

Website

The Resource Book for Teachers website, launched in April 2004, includes useful links for primary teachers, extra activities, and downloadable versions of the worksheets from this book which you can adapt for your classes. It also includes an example of an electronic portfolio (see chapter 1). The website address is: http://www.oup.com/elt/teacher/rbt

1 Language portfolios

What is a portfolio?

A language portfolio is a compilation of an individual child's work, showing his/her language abilities, effort, and language development over time. It usually includes samples of written work, audio or video recordings, drawings, teacher's notes, tests, peer- and self-assessment forms, and reviews of books read. Portfolios offer a child-friendly way of assessing language development and gaining insight into children's views, attitudes, and language-learning strategies.

Portfolios provide a way of individualizing the learning and assessment process, because each portfolio is different. The children are in control of their portfolios and can develop them in ways that express their individuality.

Portfolios encourage children's overall involvement in learning and assessment processes. Their use also affects class methodology, since portfolio-using classes usually become more child-centred and collaborative – the children and you become partners in learning. Because this empowers the children, they develop feelings of trust and respect for you as their teacher.

Nevertheless, starting to use language portfolios in your class is never altogether easy. You will need to feel comfortable with the children taking over, becoming more autonomous, and moving around the classroom. You also need to feel comfortable about inviting parents to participate in their children's learning. Most of all, you will need to be patient. Your class is not going to change overnight – the children are not going to become proficient portfolio-users in a matter of weeks. At the beginning, you will need to model every step they take, from organizing a portfolio to choosing and evaluating work samples. You, too, may need some time to experiment with the procedure, try things out, and allow yourself to make mistakes! It may help to boost your confidence if you give yourself a pilot year to try out portfolios without going through all the stages and without making them central to your assessment.

Why portfolios?

Portfolios provide you with:

– an opportunity to link instruction with assessment. You assess the children on the activities they are involved in and what is going on in the classroom;

– a record of each individual child's linguistic development, through continuous observation and information-gathering;
– a global view of the individual child's progress, including attitudes, learning strategies, interests, and talents. The children's progress can, therefore, be viewed in relation to these very important factors;
– a body of work you can use to discuss the children's progress with their parents, other teachers, the school authorities, and the children themselves;
– a reason for arranging regular conferences with each child. This way you can genuinely get to know and give particular attention to all the children and establish a strong relationship with them;
– a way of involving parents in the learning and assessment processes.

Portfolios provide the children with:
– an opportunity to become responsible for their own learning, by becoming actively involved in areas such as goal-setting and choosing and applying their assessment criteria;
– an occasion to reflect on their performance, attitudes, and personal learning styles;
– a chance to exercise some control over the assessment procedure: for example, children may have a say in choosing what pieces of work should be assessed by you and what work samples should be forwarded to the next teacher. You can also arrange times to discuss their progress and opinions with you;
– tangible evidence of progress the children can relate to, since they choose each piece they include in their portfolios;
– increased involvement in the learning process. For example, the children can suggest activities they would like to do, areas for reinforcement, or topics they would like to cover;
– increased motivation and excitement for learning. The children observe progress as it takes place, and have access to the products of their efforts to show (off!) to friends and family.

Guidelines for using portfolios

Children need some time before they can use portfolios effectively. Be patient! Try various approaches before deciding what works best for you and your children. Not everything included in this book will work for you, but we hope that you will get some ideas from it and try them out.

Above all, remember that portfolios are not collections of random pieces of work. Although you take the children's preferences into account, it is important that you set goals and include samples of work that provide evidence of the children's progress toward those goals.

Keeping and accessing portfolios

Ideally portfolios should be kept in the classroom. Choose a place the children can access easily – somewhere not too high, not behind closed or locked doors, etc. The children should feel free and able to access their portfolios whenever they wish. If classroom storage is not possible, suggest that the children take them home, or keep them in the staff room or other appropriate place at school, but the children must feel free to ask for their portfolios when they want them. You may decide to get the children to bring the portfolios to class once a week. Eventually, as more schools become equipped with computers and Internet access, the children will be able to keep on-line portfolios. This will allow them to access their portfolios from anywhere, anytime.

Confidentiality is vital because the contents of the portfolios are private. If anyone other than the child or you wants to see a portfolio, they must ask for permission. It is best if the owner of the portfolio is present when others are viewing it, except when the portfolios are being assessed by the school authorities.

Although parents are invited to view their child's portfolio at conferences with the teacher, portfolios can also be taken home if the parents are unable to come to school for the conferences, provided that they are returned promptly. The children should feel that the portfolio belongs to them. They are usually happy to share their work and their progress with parents and family.

Setting criteria for choosing work samples

Although at the beginning you will be the one choosing most of the children's work samples for inclusion in the portfolios, try to do it together with them, voicing your thoughts as to why you are choosing one piece of work and not another. Modelling the selection procedure, while also inviting the children's opinions, will put them on the road to independent selection.

Work with the children to set criteria for choosing work for their portfolios. The class can discuss and eventually identify the criteria they should be looking for, on the basis of other children's portfolios and samples of work considered good. You may start from very basic criteria but expect children to come up with more sophisticated criteria as they get more experienced. You may, therefore, need to discuss selection criteria again at a later stage of the year. Here are some criteria the children may come up with:

– I learned a lot by doing this activity.
– I enjoyed doing it.
– I think it looks nice.
– It was interesting.
– It shows that I have learned a lot.
– I haven't made many mistakes.
– My handwriting is nice.
– I like it.
– My friends think it is good.

Whatever the final list looks like, it is a good idea to type it out, perhaps in the mother tongue if necessary, copy it, and give it to each of the children to paste on the inside cover of their portfolios. As their criteria become more sophisticated, you can update the list and get them to paste it over the old one. The purpose is to remind them of the criteria when they are considering work to include in their portfolios. (See the example of a list below.)

I can add something to my portfolio when:

– I worked hard to do it.
– I enjoyed working with others (family, friends) when I did it.
– I don't have anything else like it in my portfolio.
– It's a better version of an earlier work sample.
– My teacher suggested it.
– I think it's very interesting.
– It shows I use English outside the classroom.
– It shows my English is getting better.
– I like it a lot.

Photocopiable © Oxford University Press

Our aim is to train children to reflect on their work and to make sensible decisions about what pieces of work to include in their portfolios. To help the children, try to find time to 'conference' with them to discuss their choices. A 'conference' may be a brief chat when you are looking at a new entry. If you ask the children *Why did you choose this?* and follow this up with a short discussion, it will help them to reassess their decisions and give you an insight into their selection procedures.

Nevertheless, during the selection procedure, do try to include entries that show progress towards curriculum goals. Some of your own criteria could be:
– the child wants to include the particular piece of work
– the language used is suitable to the child's language level
– the child made a significant effort in completing his/her work
– the work is a significant achievement for the child
– the work illustrates the child's strengths and positive traits.

Reviewing and updating the portfolio

Work included in the portfolio does not have to stay there permanently. Encourage the children to review their portfolios and go over their entries. This can help them to appreciate the progress they have made. You can train them to do this during one-to-one portfolio review conferences, or in model class sessions when they can review portfolio entries from past or even imaginary students.

Reviewing their portfolios and reflecting critically on their work is also important when children are choosing work samples to be passed on to their next teacher. Most of the material in their portfolio is likely to be sent home with them. Usually only a very small selection of work gets handed on to the next teacher. For this purpose, the children should choose the three or four pieces of work that best reflect their abilities and progress.

Portfolio review/assessment

A portfolio includes a wide variety of work samples offering a global view of children's progress. It includes work that demonstrates the children's progress towards the course goals: writing samples, speaking samples (tapes), assessment task results, book reports, etc. Although each child's portfolio is different, they should all provide evidence of the child's progress. The portfolio is therefore the assessment procedure that encompasses all the others and brings together assessment tasks, tests, teacher and learner-initiated work samples, reports, and teacher's and children's notes. It is the portfolio that provides an overall picture of the child. In this way, a review/assessment of the portfolio is the ultimate assessment of the child.

Portfolio assessment can take place two or three times a year, in the form of a conference between you and the child. Ideally you should get input from the children and the parents before compiling your review/report so you can include their comments in it.

Give the children time to go over their portfolios and prepare for their conference with you. If possible, invite the parents to a parent–teacher–learner conference. But if there is no time for this (you would need to allow about 30 minutes for each three-way conference), you could still get feedback by sending the parents a comment/evaluation sheet to fill in when you send home the portfolio. You can enlist the help of a colleague and take over each other's classes while you are holding reviews and conferences.

After each conference, note the comments the parents and children have made and carry out your own review of the child's portfolio. Complete your portfolio report on the basis of the work samples, assessment task results, observation notes, and comments on work samples. The sample of a review chart on the next page has been completed in note form.

A note of caution: Some parents may not be ready to accept the portfolio style of assessment. If this is the case, try using a combination of portfolio reports and traditional term reports.

Getting children and parents involved

It is vital to the success of portfolio assessment that the children are involved in all aspects of the process at all times. This involvement strengthens their feelings of ownership and responsibility for the portfolio, as well as towards the learning and assessment process in general. An additional result of being actively involved is that the

Portfolio review

Name _Alice_   **Class** _2_   **Term** _Spring_

Area	Overall achievement	Strengths	Needs and future action
Reading	Very good	– Loves books and reads a lot. – Uses pictures and context to understand unknown words.	– Needs to improve her reading speed and learn to read silently. – Should continue with readers during holidays.
Writing	Good	– Her handwriting and spelling have improved.	– Has a few problems with combining sentences. – Should practise writing short paragraphs (2–3 sentences).
Speaking	Good	– Always eager to use English. – Can talk about herself and her daily activities.	– Fluency hampered by frequent gaps in vocabulary. – Should try to increase her vocabulary.
Listening	Very good	– Can easily grasp main idea/gist of a listening text.	– Does not always recognize spoken form of words in her vocabulary. – Try listening to tapes of stories with the book open.
Attitude to English	Excellent	– Loves learning English and is always enthusiastic about her lessons.	

Teacher's signature _____   **Child's signature** _____

Parent's signature _____

children feel empowered by having control over their own learning and assessment.

Parents should also be involved in the portfolio process. They can profit from and also assist in the development of a portfolio. Being involved makes them feel part of their child's learning development and gives them an insight into what is going on in the classroom. Moreover, they can assist their children by giving positive comments on their work and by helping them to formulate selection and evaluation criteria. They can, for example, help to choose work samples for inclusion in the portfolio or offer comments on something their child has already chosen.

Here are some practical suggestions for involving children:

– Help the children to become gradually responsible for deciding what to put in their portfolios.
– Include the children as much as possible in all decision-making. When dealing with very young children, you will need to have decision-making discussions in their native language, at least for some time. The two key stages in using portfolios are formulating the selection criteria and portfolio assessment criteria. With young children who are new to the portfolio process, it may be useful to have a prepared list of criteria which you can (skilfully) elicit from them through discussion.
– Hold one-to-one conferences with the children to discuss their portfolios, assess progress, and set short-term goals such as 'I will learn to spell my name' and 'I will learn the numbers 1–20 by next month'.

And here are some practical suggestions for involving parents:

– Tell the parents, either at a meeting or by letter, how you will be using the portfolios, what the benefits are, etc.
– Invite the parents to joint parent–teacher–learner conferences on the children's progress.
– Ask the parents to fill in a form at regular intervals with comments on their children's progress. This form can eventually be included in the portfolio as well.
– Encourage parents' suggestions and comments on work samples for inclusion in their children's portfolios; these could be from the children's activities at home.

Portfolio ideas

A portfolio should include a variety of information such as assessment tasks, children's notes, journal entries, and other examples of the children's work. Very young children can report and reflect on their work and say why they want it in their portfolio in their native language. You may wish to write their comments in both languages. If the children can express themselves orally but are not able to write, help them by writing down some basic comments they dictate to you. Alternatively, use tapes to record journal entries or children's comments.

Also include your own notes and reports in the portfolio. These may consist of anecdotal accounts of something interesting that happened in class, interview notes (see the example below), a brief conversation with a child, or notes from a parent–teacher–learner conference. If you feel these should be confidential, keep them in separate portfolios to show to parents and to pass on to the children's next teacher.

Interview notes for Alice
18/4/2002

Alice and I talked about the books she likes reading. She said her parents read to her a lot. I asked her how she deals with things she doesn't understand. She said she uses pictures and the context to help her understand. She makes a lot of guesses and often these guesses are accurate.

Here we offer some some ideas to keep portfolios organized in terms of entries on rhymes, books, and children's development of extensive reading skills.

Extensive reading checklist

Keep this checklist right at the beginning of the children's portfolios for easy reference. Tell the children what the checklist is for and explain to them that it will demonstrate their progress in reading over the next two to three years. The checklist can be filled in whenever a child achieves one of the stated goals. Comments may refer to portfolio entries which offer evidence of achievement of each of those goals. You will probably need to state the goals in the native language as well as in English, so that parents can follow their children's progress and the children themselves have a record of what is expected of them next.

Extensive reading checklist

Name _____   Class _____

	Date	Comment
enjoys reading		
can identify the title and author of a reading text		
can identify the main characters		
can grasp the plot of an extensive reading text		
actively seeks opportunities to read		
can grasp the main ideas of a text		
can talk about the main characters		
reads a variety of books		
can deduce meaning from context without being obstructed by unknown words		
can summarize a text/narrate a story		
can evaluate a text		

Reading log

This is to keep track of the children's progress in extensive reading, using graded readers, etc. It is also a way for them to reflect on their work and to keep a record of their own progress in reading. The columns in the log are for the children to note when they started and when they finished reading a book. It is also a useful record of their reading speed and the interest they have shown in the books they chose.

Books are fun!

Name _____

Class _____

About the book	Started reading	Finished reading	My thoughts (What I liked/didn't like)
Book title _____ Author _____ Main characters _____ _____ _____			
Book title _____ Author _____ Main characters _____ _____ _____			

Rhyme log

This log can be used with assessment task 3.2, 'Hickory dickory dock', or by itself. Keep it in the portfolio for children to record rhymes they have learned and may have recorded on tape.

My favourite rhymes

Name _____

Class _____

Rhyme	Date recorded	My thoughts (How much I liked it/ How well I did)	My teacher's thoughts

2 Listening

Listening is vital from the first day children start learning English, whether in a formal setting in a classroom, or in a natural setting. Listening is what helps them to understand your instructions and your explanations of classroom rules and learning procedures. It is also fundamental to accessing new language and finding out how language works.

Children may take time to produce language, but this is by no means a passive phase. During this 'silent period' they are actively processing what they hear in order to understand what is being said and to find out how language works. When they feel ready, they begin to use the language actively. You can help a child in the listening stage by using pictures, gestures, and mime.

Understanding oral language is the first step towards learning. As such, it is a competence that needs to be assessed. Assessing listening comprehension gives us the first evidence that children have started making active use of their limited knowledge of the foreign language to extract meaning from what they hear. Listening assessment is the only way to find out what children really know during this silent period. Children do not necessarily need to respond verbally for you to assess whether they understand the new language. Most of the assessment tasks in this chapter are designed for children to show their understanding in non-verbal ways.

Listening as a skill consists of a variety of other sub-skills such as listening for specific information (scanning), listening for gist (skimming), listening for detailed understanding (intensive listening), guessing meaning from context, and predicting what will follow. As children become more proficient learners, they can be trained in these sub-skills to improve their ability to deal with real-life situations. A few of the assessment tasks in Chapter 2 are designed to assess the children's emergent sub-skills.

2.1   **What are they doing?**

LEVEL	**Beginners**
AGE GROUP	**6 and above**
TIME	**15–20 minutes**
DESCRIPTION	The children match photos to pictures following oral instructions.
LANGUAGE	Action verbs: *eating, drinking, painting, writing, sleeping, watching, running, listening, reading, sitting.*
SKILLS	Listening for specific information; recognizing action verbs in the present continuous.
ASSESSMENT CRITERIA	The children should be able to recognize common action verbs in spoken statements.
MATERIALS	Worksheet 2.1 (see back of book); scissors; glue; a set of photos of each of the children. If you propose to do Variation 2, you will need pictures of famous people instead. (See Variations 1 and 2.)

PREPARATION

1 Photocopy Worksheet 2.1 for each child.
2 Make a black and white photocopy of a class photo for each child or ask the children to bring in a photo of themselves which you can copy for the class. Cut out the copies so that you have a set of photos and there is a set for each of the children. If you end up with too many photos keep them to use in later activities.
3 Prepare a set of ten statements, for example, *Maria is laughing*, using the children's names and the actions in the pictures on Worksheet 2.1.

IN CLASS

1 Give out a copy of Worksheet 2.1 and a set of photos to each child.
2 Help the class decide which ten pupils' photos are to be used for the activity.
3 Tell the children to cut out the faces from the photos and stick them on the right figure according to what they hear. Tell them they will hear the sentences twice. The first time they just place the faces on the figures. They can stick them down after your second reading.
4 Read the statements you prepared, for example, *Luis is reading*, with short pauses between them.
5 Read the statements again.
6 Tell the children to stick the right face on each figure.

FEEDBACK

Ask the children to exchange worksheets and check each other's answers. Older and more confident children can then take turns to come to the front, mime the activity, and tell the class what they are doing according to the drawings, for example, *I'm Luis. I'm reading.* If the children are not able or ready to say what they are doing, they can mime the activity. If some children's pictures do not appear on the worksheet, they can say the name of a classmate and just mime the activity, for example, *Kumiko is laughing.* During this process the children check their partner's worksheets and mark them using the marking scheme below.

FOLLOW-UP

Write the sentences on the board for older children to copy under or near the appropriate figure.

VARIATION 1

1 Make a copy of Worksheet 2.1 and a set of photos of ten children in your class. In the margins of the worksheet, write the names of the ten children.

2 Give out the worksheets and tell the children that they are going to hear statements such as *Pablo is painting.* They have to draw a line to join the name and the picture showing the action. After the children have finished, check the answers with the class.

3 Then give each child the ten faces and tell them to stick the faces in the right places on the worksheet. (If this takes too long, go straight to Feedback and tell the children to stick the faces on for homework.)

VARIATION 2

This activity works well for older children using pictures of famous people instead of children's photos.

ASSESSMENT OF OUTCOME

This activity involves peer assessment and use of the discrete-point marking scheme. (See Introduction.) When they exchange worksheets, the children tick the correct answers on their partner's worksheet and then assign an overall mark, for example 8/10. They may wish to add an overall comment. Comments should be agreed on by the whole class, after discussing what constitutes 'excellent', 'very good', and 'good' performance, for example:

10 = Excellent
8–9 = Very good
6–7 = Good
0–5 = Try harder

2.2 Clothes

LEVEL	**Beginners**
AGE GROUP	**6 and above**
TIME	**15 minutes**
DESCRIPTION	The children listen and colour clothing items according to a script.
LANGUAGE	Clothes: *pyjamas, hat, sandals, dress, shorts*; colours.
SKILLS	Listening for specific information.
ASSESSMENT CRITERIA	The children should be able to recognize basic clothing items and colours in a spoken text.
MATERIALS	Worksheet 2.2 (see back of book); an enlarged photocopy of Worksheet 2.2; coloured pencils; glue; a piece of A4 paper for each child.
PREPARATION	Photocopy Worksheet 2.2 for each child. You may wish to modify the worksheet according to the needs of your class.

IN CLASS

1 Explain to the children that they are going to hear a story about clothes. They have to colour the clothes according to what they hear.

2 Give out Worksheet 2.2 and tell the story below or one of your own making.

> John and Mary are watching television. Suddenly, their dog Bruno runs in front of them. He looks very funny. Bruno is wearing **Mary's pink hat**, **blue pyjamas**, and **John's brown sandals**. Mary and John run into the bedroom. Their clothes are everywhere! **Mary's green dress** is on the floor and **John's red shorts** are on the bed. What a mess!

3 Tell the story again for the children to check or complete their work.

FEEDBACK

1 Put an enlarged copy of Worksheet 2.2 up on the board, with the clothing coloured according to the story.

2 Go round checking that the children have coloured the clothes correctly.

FOLLOW-UP

1 Give out a piece of A4 paper to each child.

2 Ask the children to cut out the clothing items on their worksheets. They then draw a boy or a girl on their piece of paper and dress him/her by pasting the appropriate clothing items on their picture.

3 Older children who are able to write can then draw lines to the clothing items and write their name and colour, for example, *a blue skirt*. If they are using textbooks, they can refer to them and copy the words they need.

4 Finally, display the children's work around the classroom before they enter it in their portfolios.

VARIATION 1

You can change the names of the characters in the story to include some of the children's names.

VARIATION 2

Adapt the story upwards or downwards to match the children's language level. If you have very young children, you will not want to expose them to language greatly beyond their level, so try using single statements, such as *Mary has a pink hat*.

ASSESSMENT OF OUTCOME

Award one point for each correctly coloured clothing item. If the children do not know the colour they can put a tick (✔) on the clothing item and score half a point for getting the clothing. Also give them half points if they identify the correct clothing item but colour it the wrong colour.

2.3   In the classroom

LEVEL

Beginners

AGE GROUP

6 and above

TIME

10 minutes

DESCRIPTION

The children listen to a series of numbered sentences and write the number of each sentence under the picture that matches it.

LANGUAGE

Classroom language: *Come here, Open your books, Sit down, Be quiet, Stand up, Stop, Listen*; numbers.

SKILLS

Listening for instructions.

ASSESSMENT CRITERIA

The children should be able to recognize spoken classroom instructions.

MATERIALS

Worksheet 2.3 (see back of book); pencils.

PREPARATION

Photocopy Worksheet 2.3 for each child.

IN CLASS

1 Give out Worksheet 2.3.

2 Tell the children to listen to you and then number the picture that matches what you said. Explain that they will hear the text twice. Warn them that some sentences will not have a matching picture.

3 Read out the following sentences, pausing after each one so that the children can mark their answers:

Number 1: Come here.
Number 2: Open your books!
Number 3: Be quiet.
Number 4: Sit down!
Number 5: Listen!
Number 6: Open your book.
Number 7: Stop.

4 Repeat the sentences.

5 Allow time for the children to check their answers.

6 Collect the worksheets for checking.

FEEDBACK

Repeat the sentences and ask the children to respond with actions or mime. You can either ask individual children or get the whole class to do the actions at the same time.

FOLLOW-UP

Let the children take your role (teacher) and give instructions to the rest of the class. The class have to respond appropriately. This could take the form of a game such as 'Simon says'.

VARIATION

Include any other instructions that you frequently use in class.

ASSESSMENT OF OUTCOME

Award two points for each correct answer.

PORTFOLIO

Children keep a list of commands or other expressions used in the classroom, for example:

• *Can you repeat please?*
• *Can I borrow a pencil?*

Help them with spelling if necessary.

2.4 Fruit fool

LEVEL

Elementary

AGE GROUP

8 and above

TIME

10 minutes

DESCRIPTION

The children listen to a recipe and scan for specific information.

LANGUAGE

Food vocabulary: *eggs, yoghurt, water, oranges, strawberries, bananas, juice, apples, bowl, kiwi, glasses, biscuits, plate, fruit*; verbs related to cooking: *mash, stir, decorate, cut, pour, add, slice; bowl, glass, fork.*

SKILLS

Listening for specific information.

ASSESSMENT CRITERIA

The children should be able to find specific information in a spoken text.

MATERIALS

Worksheet 2.4 (see back of book); overhead projector (optional); ingredients for dessert (optional).

PREPARATION

1 Photocopy Worksheet 2.4 for each child.
2 You may like to prepare a recording of the script below.
3 Set up the overhead projector if you use one.

IN CLASS

1 Give out Worksheet 2.4.
2 Tell the children that they will hear a recipe and have to tick the words they hear in part A.

Allow the children time to look at the words in part A before you start, so that they will know what to listen for. You may need to go through the vocabulary first.

3 Read the script below or play the tape.

Right, everyone. Are we ready? Today we are going to make a dessert – fruit fool. It's yummy!

You can make fruit fool with any kind of soft fruit. Today we're using strawberries or bananas.

Now, here's what we need:	Shall I say that again?
2 small bananas	2 small bananas
12 strawberries	12 strawberries
a pot of yoghurt	a pot of yoghurt
biscuits	biscuits
kiwi slices	kiwi slices
25g of sugar	25g of sugar

OK, now. Are we ready? Let's go.
1 Cut the strawberries in two, or if you are using bananas, slice them.
2 Put the fruit in a bowl and mash it with a fork.
3 Now stir the yoghurt until it is creamy.
4 Add the yoghurt and the sugar to the fruit. Stir well.
5 That's it! Pour the fruit fool into small bowls or glasses. You can decorate it with biscuits and kiwi.
Mmm … Can't wait to try it!

---

4 Tell children that they will hear the script again. This time they fill in part B, writing the numbers 1–5 in the order they hear the words.
5 Read or play the script again. Give the children a minute or so to check their answers.
6 Read the script or play the tape a final time.
7 Collect the worksheets for checking.

FEEDBACK	1 For oral feedback, put the worksheet on the overhead projector, or write it on the board, and ask the children to give you their answers.
	2 If the children are comfortable reading English, write the answers on the board.
FOLLOW-UP	If your classroom circumstances allow, bring the ingredients for the dessert and prepare the recipe in class with the children. Alternatively, give the children the recipe and suggest they make fruit fool at home. If they do, they could even bring it to the next lesson for their friends to try!
VARIATION	With a mixed ability group, you could give Part A of the activity to the weaker children and Part B to the stronger ones. Allow children to choose the task they think is most suitable to their level.
ASSESSMENT OF OUTCOME	Award one mark for each word in Part A and two marks for each word in Part B.

2.5 Crazy weather

LEVEL	**Elementary**
AGE GROUP	**10 and above**
TIME	**10 minutes**
DESCRIPTION	The children match words with pictures according to a dialogue.
LANGUAGE	Weather: *windy, cloudy, rainy, sunny, foggy, snowy*; days of the week; past tense: *was*
SKILLS	Listening for detailed information.
ASSESSMENT CRITERIA	The children should be able to understand weather vocabulary in a spoken text and recognize the days of the week.
MATERIALS	Worksheet 2.5 (see back of book); overhead projector (optional).
PREPARATION	1 Photocopy Worksheet 2.5 for each child.
	2 You may decide to record the script, with the help of friends or colleagues.
IN CLASS	1 Give out Worksheet 2.5.
	2 Tell the children they are going to hear a dialogue about Mary's holidays. They have to look at the pictures and decide which picture shows the weather on each day of her holiday.

3 Give the children plenty of time to look at the pictures.

4 Read the script below or play the tape. Pause after your reading of each day, to give the children time to find the right picture.

> **What was the weather like on Mary's holidays?**
>
> **Igor** Hi, Mary, you're back from your holidays! How was Coco Island?
>
> **Mary** It was strange! The weather was crazy. It was different every day. On Monday it was sunny…
>
> **Igor** And then?
>
> **Mary** On Tuesday it was rainy.
>
> **Igor** Really?
>
> **Mary** And on Wednesday it was very cloudy!
>
> **Igor** On Thursday?
>
> **Mary** On Thursday it was foggy.
>
> **Igor** Oh dear! And on Friday?
>
> **Mary** On Friday it was very windy, and on Saturday it snowed!
>
> **Igor** Strange! What happened on Sunday?
>
> **Mary** Oh! On Sunday, I came home.

5 Give the children a minute or so to think about their answers.

6 Read the script or play the tape again.

7 Collect the worksheets for checking.

FEEDBACK

1 Put the worksheet on the overhead projector or draw simple icons, for example, ☁ or ☀ on the board and ask the children to give you their answers, which you can write on the board. If they are able, let them come out and write the day of the week under the appropriate picture. If any of the children are not sure why they got something wrong, play or read the relevant section again.

2 If the children cannot write the days of the week, you can also call out the days for the children to mime what the weather was like on each day.

FOLLOW-UP

1 A few children can come to the front and mime weather conditions, while the rest of them guess what the weather is.

2 Ask the children to work in pairs or groups to prepare a mini play based on Mary's crazy holiday. Those children not miming the weather can take the part of scenery, such as trees, animals, etc.

VARIATION

By varying the vocabulary, you can do the same task with various sports or animals, for example, what the children did everyday at a sports camp, or what they saw during a safari trip in the jungle.

ASSESSMENT OF OUTCOME

Award two marks for each question answered correctly.

3 Speaking

Speaking can be the most rewarding and motivating skill, especially for children, who get excited when they are able to express a few things in the target language. They want to go home able to sing a song or recite a rhyme, and are eager to show off their new-found ability to their family and friends. Nevertheless, speaking can also be frightening and intimidating for shy children. It requires great care in the choice of speaking-assessment tasks and overall assessment procedure, to ensure that children have opportunities to perform in ways and situations that are informal and non-threatening. Give them opportunities to work and speak in pairs or groups, and to speak individually only when they are ready. Speaking-assessment tasks must also be realistic (i.e. realistic and genuine communicative interactions) and contextualized (i.e. in contexts familiar and interesting to the children).

In this chapter we offer a variety of examples of how to assess speaking on the basis of these criteria. We suggest marking schemes relevant to the children's language levels, as well as self- and peer-assessment, journal writing, interviews, and portfolios. See Chapter 10 for marking schemes for speaking.

For the class teacher, the main problem in assessing speaking is dealing with the practicalities. How does one assess speaking in a class of 30 or more children whom one sees maybe twice a week? One solution is to get the whole class to prepare for the speaking assessment, but only choose one group of four to six children to assess at a time. The number of children you assess depends on the task and the time required for it (the more time you have, the more children you can assess), and on how experienced you are (the more experienced you become, the faster you will be able to assess the children). Keep a record of which children you have assessed until you have covered the entire class.

Once you have started the assessment task and the children are working smoothly, you can concentrate on the group you are assessing, making notes if you need to (discreetly, so that you don't upset the children). Assign silent follow-up activities, so that fast finishers are kept busy and allow you time to finish the assessment. If you use the relevant Speaking report forms (see 10.4 and 10.9), you will have the aims of your assessment handy, and when you fill it in, you immediately have a completed report to give to the children. Make sure you fill in the form as soon as possible after the lesson, so that you can still remember which child did what! When you give the children their reports, try to give them more oral feedback and encouragement on their performance.

You can assess a larger number of children, possibly all of them, if you use a cassette to record them while they are carrying out the speaking task. Recording the assessment allows you to listen to the children in your own time and also provides a permanent record for the children's portfolio.

By observing just four to six children at a time, you might worry that the rest of the class feels cheated, because they prepared for the task but have not been assessed. You can get round this in a way that satisfies the children. Ask all the children, including the ones you have assessed, to use self- or peer-assessment at the end of the task. Then find time to collect and look at their self-assessments and discuss them briefly. You can keep some comments on the discussion and add them to their portfolio together with their self-assessment and their own comments.

In addition, children can also write comments on their performance, their feelings, even on the task itself in their journals. (See 8.7, 'Journal writing'.)

3.1   Getting to know you

LEVEL	**Beginners**
AGE GROUP	**6 and above**
TIME	**15 minutes**
DESCRIPTION	This is an information-gap activity. The children ask and answer questions to obtain personal information.
LANGUAGE	Question formation and asking for personal information: *What's your name? How old are you? What's your favourite …?*
SKILLS	Speaking: asking and answering questions; providing personal information.
ASSESSMENT CRITERIA	The children should be able to ask questions to get personal information, provide information about themselves, carry out the task successfully, use basic turn-taking skills, and work with others.
MATERIALS	Worksheet 3.1 (see next page); overhead projector (optional)
PREPARATION	Photocopy Worksheet 3.1 for each child.
IN CLASS	1 Write Worksheet 3.1 on the board, or put it up on the overhead projector.
	2 Explain to the children that they have to fill in this form by asking four of their classmates questions. Make sure they ask children they don't sit with or know too well.

3 Tell them that they can get up and walk around the room to find the four classmates and talk to them. Ask them not to make too much noise or disturb others. If you have a very large class, have the children sit at a different place than usual. Then they can ask classmates near them and not have to walk around.

4 If there is any information they are unable to write (such as a surname), they can ask their classmate to spell it for them. If the children need help but don't know how to ask for it, write the relevant question on the board for them to refer to (for example 'How do you spell …?').

5 Give out Worksheet 3.1.

Worksheet 3.1

Getting to know you

Name _____ Class _____ Date _____

Choose four friends. Ask them questions and complete the form. Use English!

Friend 1   **Friend 2**

Name _____   Name _____

Age _____   Age _____

Favourite food _____   Favourite food _____

Favourite colour _____   Favourite colour _____

Favourite … _____   Favourite … _____

Friend 3   **Friend 4**

Name _____   Name _____

Age _____   Age _____

Favourite food _____   Favourite food _____

Favourite colour _____   Favourite colour _____

Favourite … _____   Favourite … _____

6 The children go round asking their classmates questions, then fill in the form.

FEEDBACK

1 Invite children to tell you how they think they did, what difficulties they experienced, and how they dealt with them. Then give general feedback on how well you think they carried out the task, for example, how polite they were, whether they used only English, etc. Tell them gently how they can improve, focusing on the general aims of the activity (see Assessment Criteria above) and not on accuracy.

2   When all the children have finished, ask them to look at their worksheets and choose one piece of information they didn't know about one of their classmates. The children take turns to say what they learnt, for example, *Conchita's favourite food is pizza*.

3   If you have chosen to observe and assess a small group of children (see introduction to this chapter), give them more detailed feedback on how they performed, in private. If you can't find time for individual conferencing, have a group conference with these children. Base your feedback on 10.9, 'Speaking task report A', which includes the marking scheme and a report on speaking.

ASSESSMENT OF OUTCOME

Select a number of children to observe while they are carrying out the task. Use 10.9a, 'Speaking task report', to assess and report on their achievement. All the children complete self-assessment form 8.8.

PORTFOLIO

The children prepare a visual presentation about their classmates or a group of friends. Depending on their level, they include information on name, age, birthday, etc. If possible they should bring a picture of their classmates/friends to accompany the report. Alternatively, they can draw their picture.

3.2   Hickory dickory dock

LEVEL

Beginners

AGE GROUP

6 and above

TIME

One week

DESCRIPTION

The children practise reciting a nursery rhyme at home. When they think they have mastered it, they record themselves and bring the tape to you.

LANGUAGE

Telling the time: This rhyme does not test any particular language item, but can be learnt when the class is practising time. Choose other rhymes according to your syllabus. Some suggestions are:

– 'Polly put the kettle on' for imperatives
– 'Incy-wincy spider' for weather vocabulary
– 'Hey diddle diddle' for vocabulary. The children can change the animals in the rhyme or add new ones. For *dish* and *spoon*, substitute animals.
– 'There was an old woman' for past simple (older children).

SKILLS

Speaking: intonation and pronunciation.

ASSESSMENT CRITERIA

The children should be able to recite a specific nursery rhyme with acceptable pronunciation and intonation.

MATERIALS

A worksheet with the rhyme; cassette; blank tapes; peer-assessment forms.

PREPARATION

1 Ask each child to bring a blank tape to class.
2 Prepare a worksheet with the rhyme for each child.
3 (Optional) Record yourself or another person reciting the rhyme. Make a copy for each of the children, using their tapes.
4 Copy a few peer-assessment forms for each child for future use (see page 49).

IN CLASS

1 Tell the children they are going to learn a rhyme by heart, and that they have a week to do this.
2 Give out the worksheet to each child.
3 Read out the rhyme or play the tape to the class.
4 Read or play it again. Then get the children to join in. Repeat the rhyme as many times as necessary. Add some actions and movements to help the children to memorize the rhyme, for example:

Hickory dickory dock.	*The children clap three times.*
The mouse ran up the clock.	*They walk their fingers up their arm.*
The clock struck one,	*They clap once.*
The mouse ran down.	*They walk their fingers down their arm.*
Hickory dickory dock.	*The children clap three times.*

5 With younger children, you could give them a drawing of a mouse and a grandfather clock to cut out. They could then move the mouse up and down the clock as they recite the rhyme.
6 Explain to the children that you are going to assess them on how well they say this rhyme at the end of the week. Give them the deadline date and reassure them that they just have to do their best. Tell them to practise at home by comparing themselves with the recording. When they feel ready, they record themselves on the tape and bring it back to you.
7 If the parents are able to help, try to involve them, too. Tell the children that they can ask their parents or other family members to listen to them reciting the rhyme and to comment on their performance. When the children are ready to record, they may need help from their parents to operate the record function on the cassette recorder.

8 Let those children who feel confident enough to say the rhyme in class do so. If any children are not happy reciting aloud, you can listen to their tape in private later.

9 Listening to anything up to 30 rhymes at one sitting is likely be too much for even the most enthusiastic rhyme-lovers. If a lot of children want to recite their rhyme in class, spread their performances over two or three lessons.

FEEDBACK

1 If you assess the children on the basis of the recording, make notes while you listen to the tape and give private feedback to each child later.

2 If a child has recited his/her rhyme in class, feedback can be through peer-assessment (see Assessment of Outcome below). Also try to find time to discuss each child's peer-assessment forms and give your own feedback.

VARIATION 1

If you don't have access to a cassette player, the final goal could be voluntary oral presentation of the rhyme in class. Make it possible for shy children to recite their rhyme to you privately before or after class. In order to help them with the practising stage, you can recite the rhyme in class each lesson during the preparation period.

VARIATION 2

Each child can choose a rhyme he/she likes and work with that one so that the class gets a variety of rhymes to listen to.

ASSESSMENT OF OUTCOME

1 If a child performs in front of the class, you can use peer-assessment. Use the peer-assessment form on the next page. Each performance doesn't have to be assessed by all peers.

2 Divide the class into groups of three or four. Each child is then assessed by one of the groups (not the one he/she belongs to). Each child thus carries out four assessments for his/her classmates and collects four assessment forms with comments about his/her own performance.

3 If you are going to be the only one listening to a rhyme, assign a mark/comment holistically according to the impression you get from the performance. Emphasize pronunciation and intonation. You could also ask the parents to give a grade/comment.

PORTFOLIO

1 Include the child's tape, together with your notes on the child's performance and peer-assessment forms. A note written in the mother tongue by the parents and/or child with their thoughts on the activity (how well he/she did or how he/she enjoyed it) can also be included with the tape.

2 Recommend to those children who enjoyed this activity that they continue recording the rhymes they like, either from among those you introduce in class or others they learn from other sources. The children should feel free to ask for your help whenever they need it and bring the tape back to you each time they add a new

My name _____

Name of rhyme _____

Date _____

Rhyme read out by _____

1 I loved listening to the rhyme.   Very Good. ☐

2 I liked listening to the rhyme.   Good. ☐

3 Listening to the rhyme was OK but it could be better.   Try Harder. ☐

Photocopiable © Oxford University Press

rhyme. Your regular encouragement, in the form of private comments or public appreciation, will keep the children interested in the project. If children do this, they can use the Rhyme Log from Chapter 1, page 33.

3.3 Monster differences

LEVEL Beginners

AGE GROUP 8 and above

TIME 20 minutes

DESCRIPTION This is an information-gap activity in which children colour pictures and then find the differences between them.

LANGUAGE Question formation and parts of the body: *arms, legs, head, eyes, ears, teeth, hands*; *How many … has … got?*; colours: *What colour is/are …?*; numbers.

SKILLS Speaking: asking and answering questions.

ASSESSMENT CRITERIA The children should be able to ask and answer simple questions, work co-operatively in pairs, and carry out the task successfully.

MATERIALS

Worksheet 3.3 (see back of book); coloured pencils; overhead projector (optional); a piece of A4 paper for each child (optional).

PREPARATION

1 Photocopy Worksheet 3.3, one for each pair of children. Copy the score sheet below for each child. Remind the children to bring their coloured pencils.

2 Cut the worksheets in two and give one half to each child of a pair.

3 Set up the overhead projector if you are using one.

4 If you use the Variation, get the children to prepare monster drawings ahead of time.

IN CLASS

1 Tell the children you are going to give each of them a picture of a monster to colour. Point out that each child will have a different monster from his/her partner's.

2 When they have coloured their monsters, they have to work with a partner, asking each other questions to find the differences between their monsters.

3 Write the words the children will need on the board for them to refer to, for example, *eyes, ears, arms, legs, teeth*; *How many heads/eyes/ears/arms/legs has your monster got?*

4 Give out Worksheet 3.3 and allow the children time to colour their monsters.

5 If you think it necessary, demonstrate the activity to the class. Colour your own monster either on your own worksheet or on a transparency. Invite a volunteer to work with you so that you can find the differences between his/her monster and yours. If you choose a strong learner, this can help the rest of the class because they see how the task is carried out. If you don't use an overhead projector, make sure to show your completed worksheet to the children, so they can see the differences for themselves.

6 Monitor the class while they are colouring and ask them not to spend time colouring in too carefully. This can cause problems if some children have finished and their partners are still colouring. If this happens, tell the children who are still colouring to decide what colour they want the hair, arms, etc. to be and just to put the right coloured dots on the different parts of their picture. They can finish colouring later if they want to.

7 Put the children into pairs. Make sure that they change partners, so that they are not sitting next to the child who saw them colouring.

8 Get the children started on finding the differences. Remind them not to look at each other's worksheets.

FEEDBACK

This activity involves self-assessment. When each pair has finished, they can look at each other's monster. They can then assess how well they've done and give themselves a score based on the score sheet

Monster differences

We checked our monsters and there are _____ differences.

The differences are:

1 _____   6 _____

2 _____   7 _____

3 _____   8 _____

4 _____   9 _____

5 _____   10 _____

We found _____ differences.   We get _____ points.

Signatures _____   _____

on this page. They should write down the differences in note form, for example, 1 = green hair, 2 = three legs, etc.

FOLLOW-UP

The children pretend to be one of the monsters, give themselves a name, and introduce themselves in two or three sentences. For example:

Hi, I'm Scary! I have two heads and five legs. My hair is green.

VARIATION

You can lower the language level for this activity by limiting the language used as well as the number of differences. For example, if the children don't colour their monsters, the questions will be *How many teeth/ears/eyes/arms/legs has it got?* and there will only be five differences focused on.

ASSESSMENT OF OUTCOME

1 Choose two or three pairs of children to observe while the rest are carrying out the activity. Use assessment Worksheet 10.9a, 'Speaking Task Report'.

2 The children can also check their own performance by using the score sheet for self-assessment.

PORTFOLIO

If the children want to, they can include their worksheets with the coloured monsters and their score sheet in their portfolios.

3.4 Look at my room

LEVEL	**Elementary**
AGE GROUP	**8 and above**
TIME	**15–20 minutes**

DESCRIPTION

The children work in pairs to describe a room. Each child places household objects on a worksheet according to the other's description.

LANGUAGE

Prepositions: *in, on, under, in front of, between, next to, above, below; top, bottom, left, right, corner; there is/are*; household objects and furniture.

SKILLS

Speaking: describing a room.

ASSESSMENT CRITERIA

The children should be able to describe a room, work co-operatively in pairs, and carry out the task successfully.

MATERIALS

Worksheet 3.4; coloured pencils; scissors; glue; a piece of A4 paper for each child; self-assessment forms.

PREPARATION

1 Photocopy Worksheet 3.4: two copies for each child.
2 If you want to save time, give out the worksheets beforehand and ask the children to cut out the objects at home and bring them to class in an envelope.

IN CLASS

1 Give out Worksheet 3.4. Ask the children to cut out the household objects on the worksheets.
2 Each child places the objects on one of his/her room plans. Make sure that the children do not look at each other's worksheets. If this is impossible, get them to change partners before they start working in pairs.
3 Put the children in pairs. When they are ready, they take turns to describe their room. Their partner positions the second set of objects on their second worksheet according to the description they hear. Encourage the children to ask questions if they need help.
4 Go round monitoring the activity to make sure all the pairs are working well.

FEEDBACK

1 The children check each other's worksheets and clear up possible misunderstandings.
2 To get an overall idea of the class' performance, hold a teacher-led session in which you ask questions such as:
  – *Who got everything right?*
  – *How many did you get right?*
  etc.

FOLLOW-UP	1 The children can colour the objects and paste them onto the worksheet. Older children could also write a simple description of the room on a separate paper. Put the children's work on display around the classroom.
	2 If the children have written a description of the room, take in the descriptions. Put the pictures on the board and then give out the descriptions randomly to the children. Each child reads the description he/she receives and then has to find the corresponding picture.
ASSESSMENT OF OUTCOME	1 Use 10.9a, 'Speaking Task Report'. Give special emphasis to the children's task achievement and their communicative competence. This will be reflected in the outcome of the task.
	2 You can also use a discrete-point marking scheme, awarding a mark for every object correctly placed.
	3 All the children should complete self-assessment form 8.8 (page 121).

3.5 Who's got my shopping?

LEVEL	**Elementary**
AGE GROUP	**10 and above**
TIME	**15–20 minutes**
DESCRIPTION	The children work in groups of four, asking and answering questions to carry out a task.
LANGUAGE	Question formation and shopping vocabulary: *bananas, apples, cat food, shampoo, soap, lamp, chocolate cake, ketchup, pencil, milk, water, lemonade, orange juice, chocolates, sweets, sandwich, crisps, biscuits, jam, chicken, Have you got a/an …? Have you got any …? Yes! No! Here you are. Thank you.*
SKILLS	Speaking: asking and answering yes/no questions.
ASSESSMENT CRITERIA	The children should be able to form comprehensible questions and answers and use turn-taking skills. Their language need not be completely accurate, but should convey the desired message and contribute to the solution of the task.
MATERIALS	Worksheet 3.5 (see back of book); pencils; cassette (optional); an individual silent activity for fast finishers.
PREPARATION	1 Photocopy Worksheet 3.5 for each group of four and cut it into sections a, b, c, and d.

2   Make sure you have an individual silent activity you can give out to fast finishers.

IN CLASS

1   Divide the class into groups of four.

2   Give out one picture to each child so that each group has pictures a, b, c, and d.

3   Explain to the children that they go shopping and literally bump into their friends. All their bags fall onto the floor and their shopping gets mixed up. When they put things back in their bags, they need to see if they have the right things.

4   Tell the children that each person has their bag and their shopping list. They have first to find out what things are missing. Then they ask the others if they have the missing items. Whenever they find an item, they put a tick on their list and carry on until they have recovered everything.

5   Draw a bag and a shopping list on the board and show what things are missing from the bag. Put a question mark (?) next to the things that are missing.

6   Give the children time to look at their worksheets and put a question mark (?) next to the things missing from their bags.

7   Use the list on the board to act out the situation with one of the stronger children. Depending on the ability of the children, it may be necessary to write the dialogue on the board:

Teacher: Have you got any apples?
Child: No.
Teacher: Have you got a chocolate cake?
Child: Yes. Here you are.
Teacher: Thank you.

8   Tell the children to begin the task.

9   Go round monitoring the activity to make sure all the groups are working well.

10 Give out a silent activity to the fast finishers, so that the rest have a chance to finish their task.

FEEDBACK

1   When all the children have finished, ask them to stop what they are doing (the written follow-up activity) and report to the class. Ask how many of them managed to find all the missing items from their lists. Congratulate them accordingly.

2   Ask a group of four confident children to the front to do the task again. The others listen and compare the way their group went about the task. Ask the other groups to say if they had any difficulties, how easy/difficult it was for them, what they did well, and how they could do better.

3   If the children feel comfortable recording their voices, you could give one or two groups a cassette to record their work. You could then play the recorded task to the rest of the class. Again ask the other groups for comments.

FOLLOW-UP	1 Younger children could work in groups and play a memory/speaking game. The first member of the group says 'I want to buy a banana'. The second player has to repeat the same sentence and add one more item: 'I want to buy a banana and cake', and so forth. (If you are using food vocabulary, make sure you pre-set the vocabulary for singular countables, so that the children don't have to cope with *some* and *any*. Also practise *a/an* beforehand.) The group scores a point for every child who says the sentence correctly. The group with the most points is the winner.
	2 Older children can follow up the activity with written work such as word puzzles or other vocabulary games that focus on the vocabulary items you are assessing.
ASSESSMENT OF OUTCOME	1 Concentrate on one or two groups to observe. If you used cassettes you can also concentrate on the groups you recorded. Use 10.9b, 'Speaking Task Report' to assess the children in the selected groups and report on their progress.
	2 All the children should complete self-assessment form 8.8.

3.6 They're the best

LEVEL	Elementary
AGE GROUP	8 and above
TIME	10 minutes
DESCRIPTION	The children ask and answer questions to complete cards about famous football players.
LANGUAGE	Question formation: *What's his name/surname? Where's he from? How tall is he? How old is he?*
SKILLS	Speaking: asking for and giving information.
ASSESSMENT CRITERIA	The children should be able to ask and answer questions on basic personal facts about famous people, carry out the task successfully, and work co-operatively in pairs.
MATERIALS	Worksheets 3.6a and b (see back of book); cassette; tapes; overhead projector (optional).
PREPARATION	1 Photocopy Worksheets 3.6a and 3.6b for each pair of children. 2 (Optional) Ask the children to bring a tape each to class.

IN CLASS	1 Divide the children into pairs.
	2 Give out Worksheets 3.6a and 3.6b face down to each pair.
	3 Ask the children to turn their worksheets over and look at them. Stress that they must not look at their partner's worksheet.
	4 Tell them that they have to fill in the missing information by asking their partner questions.
	5 While they work, go round checking that all the pairs are working smoothly.
FEEDBACK	1 When all the children have finished, copy the worksheets onto the board or put the them on the overhead projector.
	2 Invite volunteer pairs to ask and answer questions until all five cards are complete.
FOLLOW-UP	1 Ask for volunteers to use the completed information on their worksheets to make an oral presentation about one of the football players.
	2 Older children may like to prepare a role play in pairs. Each pair acts out the parts of a journalist and a famous football player. Their questions will be based on the card, but also allow them to use their imagination or background knowledge to add more questions or new information.
VARIATION 1	Give half the class the completed versions of the cards and the other half empty ones. The children with the empty ones interview the others and fill in the cards.
VARIATION 2	You can do the same activity using the children's favourite singers, actors, or basketball players. Older children might like to do the activity with more demanding information about their favourite artists or historical figures. The children can bring their own knowledge to the task if you ask them to look up information about their favourite footballer/singer/actor, etc. You could give them a list of things to research, for example height, birthday, etc. When they bring the information to you, you can choose which people to include and create new worksheets accordingly.
ASSESSMENT OF OUTCOME	Use 10.9a, 'Speaking Task Report', for those you have observed, and have all the children complete self-assessment form 8.8. Then invite them to write comments on their performance and write up the task in their journals. Respond to their comments with messages in their journals.
PORTFOLIO	1 While the children carry out the task you may, with their permission, record them and include the tape in their portfolios. The same can be done with the Follow-up activities.
	2 The children can add any material they found on their favourite athlete or famous figure to their portfolio. This could be the start of a collection of authentic target language material.

4 Reading

Good readers enjoy reading, get better at it, read more, and consequently improve both their reading skills and their general language ability. When children have difficulties with reading, however, they start to dislike it, read less, don't improve, and consequently have more reading problems and grow to dislike it even more. To prevent spiralling negative attitudes, we need to help children to improve their reading skills and learn to enjoy reading from the very beginning.

One way to help children improve their reading skills is to train them to use the sub-skills involved, such as skimming and scanning. Poor readers have often learnt only one style of reading, usually intensive reading. The inability to differentiate between reading skills usually makes readers slow and dependent on every single word they read, whereas good readers are fast, and are able to predict content and guess the meaning of words from the overall context of the passage. These are skills that can be developed by training.

Because we believe that assessment should be a continuation of the work done in the classroom, we recommend that reading assessment be done in an interesting, contextualized, fun, and authentic way. We have also included assessment of extensive reading. Even though it has been argued that extensive reading should not be assessed because it diminishes the children's enjoyment and can eventually put them off reading altogether, our argument is that it is an important skill and an invaluable learning resource. If it is assessed in a positive and child-friendly way it will not create negative feelings in children. On the contrary, it can help them realize that it is important and may result in more extensive reading in the English lesson.

4.1 Problems at the zoo

LEVEL	**Beginners**
AGE GROUP	**6 and above**
TIME	**10 minutes**
DESCRIPTION	The children match words with pictures.
LANGUAGE	Animal names: *fox, lion, elephant, pony, crocodile, giraffe, hippo, snake, gorilla, penguin*

SKILLS	Reading: recognizing animal words.
ASSESSMENT CRITERIA	The children should be able to recognize the written form of selected vocabulary items.
MATERIALS	Worksheets 4.1a and b (see back of book); an enlarged copy of the worksheet; A3 card to make a set of cards with the names of the animals; Blu-Tack; prize stickers (optional)

PREPARATION

1 Photocopy Worksheets 4.1a and b for each child.
2 Prepare a set of cards with the vocabulary you are assessing.

IN CLASS

1 Give out Worksheet 4.1a to each child.
2 Explain in the mother tongue that there has been a big storm and that all the letters have fallen off the signs at the zoo. They have to put the signs back by drawing lines to match the signs with the animals.

FEEDBACK

1 Put the enlarged worksheet on the board. Hand out the animal name cards you made. Invite the children with the cards to come out and take turns sticking the words on the right signs.
2 Go round the class and check that the children are correcting their work. If one of the children at the board makes a mistake, make sure the others point it out in a calm, friendly, and non-threatening way and that he/she is given a second chance before another child gives the answer.
3 When the children have finished the activity and their self-assessment (see Assessment of Outcome below), discuss how they know when they are 'doing well' and when they 'need to work harder'.

FOLLOW-UP

1 The children play a memory game, using the names of all the animals they have learnt up to now. The game can be played either with the whole class or in groups of five or six.
2 One child starts by saying the name of an animal, for example, *a lion*. The next child repeats the animal already mentioned and adds another one for example, *a lion and a penguin*. The next adds another, and so on, until a child can't name another animal or until the last child repeats everyone else's animals, adds his/her own, and wins.

VARIATION 1

When you are going to assess animal words, ask the children to name their favourites. You can decide to assess those instead of the ones listed above. If the children come up with a lot of animals, you might decide together on which names should be assessed.

VARIATION 2

You can also use this task to assess copying skills if you ask the children to copy the words on the appropriate sign rather than draw a line. In this case make sure that your marking reflects what you are testing, in this case reading and writing. (You could allocate half or a quarter of the marks to copying, depending on the importance you attach to this skill).

ASSESSMENT OF OUTCOME

1 Self-assessment. Give out Worksheet 4.1b and a set of prize stickers, one to each child (optional).

2 While the feedback is going on at the board, the children assess themselves by placing a 'happy' sticker under each word they got right or a sad sticker under each word they got wrong. If you don't have stickers, the children can draw happy/sad faces.

3 Monitor the children and make sure they are able to do the self-assessment. Provide help where needed.

4 If at the feedback stage you discussed 'doing well', the children can write a final comment for themselves. You can decide on the criteria with the children, for example:

8–10 correct answers (Very good!)
6–7 correct answers (Good!)
3–5 correct answers (Be careful.)
0–2 correct answers (You need to try harder.)

5 The children can take the worksheets and the assessment forms home to share their achievements with their parents.

PORTFOLIO

1 Once the worksheets have been returned, the children may want to include them in their portfolios along with their self-assessment forms.

2 If the children are using self-assessment 8.3, 'A picture of achievement', they can now add the animals in the picture as proof of having learnt the names.

4.2 Zinky's home

LEVEL

Beginners

AGE GROUP

6 and above

TIME

10 minutes

DESCRIPTION

The children read sentences and use the appropriate colours to colour a picture.

LANGUAGE

Nature vocabulary: *flowers, sky, grass, river, clouds, trees, cows*; colours.

SKILLS

Reading: comprehending simple sentences.

ASSESSMENT CRITERIA	The children should be able to recognize the written form of colours in a simple text and understand short written sentences with known vocabulary.
MATERIALS	Worksheet 4.2 (see back of book); coloured pencils; coloured chalks or whiteboard markers; prize stickers (optional)

PREPARATION

1 Photocopy Worksheet 4.2 for each child.
2 Prepare a class set of Worksheet 4.2 without the text for the Follow-up.

IN CLASS

1 Explain in the mother tongue that they have got a postcard from an alien called Zinky.
2 Draw 'Zinky' on the board and introduce her to the children. Zinky has asked them to colour her postcard so that they understand what her planet looks like.
3 Give out Worksheet 4.2 to each child.
4 Tell the children to read the text and colour the picture.

FEEDBACK

1 Draw a rough outline of the picture on the board. When the children have finished, invite volunteers to come out one at a time to colour part of the picture. Start with the weaker volunteers so that they have more choice and can colour the parts they know. Gradually the picture will be complete and the children can compare their own with the one on the board.
2 Then ask the children to do self-assessment (see Assessment of Outcome below).
3 If any children get a colour wrong, find out whether they know the colour in their mother tongue.

FOLLOW-UP

1 Give out Worksheet 4.2 without the text and ask the children to colour it with the colours we have here on Earth.
2 They can then write the colour on the appropriate areas of the picture (for example *green* on the grass, *white* on the clouds, etc.), or copy Zinky's sentences, but change the colours. They can then send their own postcard to outer space!

VARIATION 1

With very young children, if they know the colours but not the rest of the vocabulary, you can assess colours by omitting the text and adding arrows with the words indicating what colour each object should be.

VARIATION 2

1   If the class has one or two computers, you could create the picture on the class computer (using Paint or a similar program) and save it as a template. The children complete the task at their own pace or when assigned to do so by you. They save the file under their name and read the instructions/text.

2   They then colour the shapes by clicking on the right colour and the right place in the picture.

3   Finally, they print out the completed picture when they have finished.

4   If you have access to a computer lab all the children can do it at the same time.

ASSESSMENT OF OUTCOME

1   Self-assessment. To carry out their assessment, give the children prize stickers (hearts, suns, stars, etc.) or ask them to draw stars next to the appropriate sentence on the Worksheet for each colour they got right. There are eight colours in the text.

2   Finally, the children give themselves a grade/comment according to the scheme you write on the board:

8 stars = Excellent!
6–7 stars = Very good!
4–5 stars = Good!
0–3 stars = Try harder.

PORTFOLIO

1   This is something the children may want to keep in their portfolio. Ask them if they do. If children who didn't do well are reluctant to put the worksheets in their portfolio, give them the opportunity to complete the follow-up activity and include that instead or as well.

2   The children can add a comment such as 'I know the colours'.

3   If the children are using self-assessment 8.3, 'A picture of achievement', they can now add the rainbow as proof of having learnt the colours.

4.3 Messages on the fridge

LEVEL	**Beginners**
AGE GROUP	**6 and above**
TIME	**10 minutes**
DESCRIPTION	The children match instructions with pictures.
LANGUAGE	Giving instructions: use of imperatives.
SKILLS	Reading: comprehending written instructions.
ASSESSMENT CRITERIA	The children should be able to understand short written instructions.
MATERIALS	Worksheet 4.3 (see back of book); small pieces of paper for each child.
PREPARATION	Photocopy Worksheet 4.3 for each child.

IN CLASS

1 Give out Worksheet 4.3 to each child.
2 Tell the children to imagine that they go home and there is nobody there. They find a lot of messages on the fridge. They manage to do everything, so a friend draws pictures of what they have done to show their parents. They have to match each message with the right picture.
3 Collect the worksheets for checking.

FEEDBACK

1 Call out the number alongside one of the pictures. Ask a volunteer to come out and mime what is happening in the picture. The rest have to guess which message it is and say it out loud.
2 Write it up on the board and put the right picture number next to it.

FOLLOW-UP

1 Give out a piece of paper to each child.
2 The children write an instruction, for example *Drink your milk!* Help them where necessary.
3 They fold the piece of paper and hand it to you. Mix all the papers up.
4 The children take turns to come out and pick one of the papers. They read their paper silently, then mime carrying out the instruction. The rest of the class have to guess the instruction and say it out loud.

5 For very young children who are not able to write yet, prepare a set of instructions and put them in a hat. The children can then pick papers out of the hat, read them, and mime the instructions.

VARIATION 1	If you would like older children to contribute towards their assessment, ask them to write an instruction each. You can then randomly select five or ten and prepare a worksheet to assess those.
VARIATION 2	If you want to assess the children's ability to form the imperative, you could erase the messages on the fridge and ask the children to come and write up the missing messages.
ASSESSMENT OF OUTCOME	Use a discrete-point marking scheme. Assign two points out of ten for each correct match.

4.4 Grandma's garden

LEVEL	**Elementary**
AGE GROUP	**8 and above**
TIME	**15 minutes**
DESCRIPTION	The children complete a picture based on a written passage.
LANGUAGE	Prepositions: *in, on, under, in front of; there is; there are.*
SKILLS	Intensive reading; writing (in Follow-up).
ASSESSMENT CRITERIA	The children should be able to comprehend a short written passage in detail.
MATERIALS	Worksheet 4.4 (see back of book); an enlarged photocopy of the worksheet.
PREPARATION	1 Photocopy Worksheet 4.4 for each child. 2 Complete the picture and make an enlarged photocopy for the Feedback.
IN CLASS	1 Give out Worksheet 4.4. 2 Ask the children to read the passage and draw the five things missing from the picture.
FEEDBACK	1 Put the enlarged photocopy of the completed drawing up on the board. 2 Ask the children to check their work and assess themselves (see Assessment of Outcome below). Monitor this process, offering help when needed.

3 When the children have finished, discuss their performance to see if they are happy with their results, whether they think they could have done better, and why they think they made mistakes, etc.

FOLLOW-UP	As a writing follow-up, get each child to draw two new items on their picture and then complete the text accordingly.
VARIATION 1	The text can be adapted to the level of the class or the prepositions you want to assess by adding or eliminating items.
VARIATION 2	The children can prepare similar texts and exchange them with their peers. Each child completes his/her partner's picture.
ASSESSMENT OF OUTCOME	Use a discrete-point marking scheme. Allocate two points for each correct addition.

4.5   A cartoon strip

LEVEL	**Elementary**
AGE GROUP	**8 and above**
TIME	**20–30 minutes**
DESCRIPTION	The children prepare a cartoon strip based on one scene or the overall plot of a story or reader they have read.
LANGUAGE	Involves the children's overall linguistic ability.
SKILLS	Extensive reading: comprehending extensive texts.
ASSESSMENT CRITERIA	The children should be able to understand a written story.
MATERIALS	Graded readers or story-books, markers, coloured pencils; a piece of paper or card for each child.
PREPARATION	Give the children a number of story-books or readers to choose from well in advance.
IN CLASS	1 The children choose a book they have read and want to work on. Explain that they have to draw a cartoon strip based either on one particular scene or on the overall plot of the story. They also have to add speech bubbles or write captions for the pictures they draw.
	2 Remind the children of the basic conventions for cartoon strips:
	– The progression is always from left to right and from top to bottom.
	– Speech bubbles at the top of the frames are read before the lower ones.

3 Give a piece of paper or card to each child and tell them to start.

4 Go round monitoring the activity, helping when necessary.

FEEDBACK

Comment on the children's cartoon strips individually.

FOLLOW-UP 1

Ask the children to prepare an alternative scene or ending to the story in their cartoon.

FOLLOW-UP 2

1 The children get together in groups, have a look at each others' cartoons, and select one.

2 They then mime the scene in the cartoon to the class. The class have to guess which scene it is and/or which reader it comes from. (This is only possible if all children in the class are familiar with the same readers.)

VARIATION 1

If the children cannot write, so cannot complete speech bubbles, accept drawings instead. Check the children's understanding by talking to them in the mother tongue.

VARIATION 2

1 You can turn this activity into a take-home test. This will save you valuable class time and give the children the benefit of increased autonomy. You can follow the steps described in In Class above.

2 Remind the children that a take-home test is their responsibility and that they are expected to carry it out themselves. But they can show their work to their parents or other family to get feedback. The final feedback can be a note from the parents stapled onto the cartoon when it is returned to you.

3 Also ask the children to add their own comments, including mention of any help they had from others.

4 Finally, agree a deadline with the children for handing in the work. You can help the parents by sending a note to them explaining what a take-home test is and what is expected of them.

ASSESSMENT OF OUTCOME

1 Assess the activity on the extent to which the children have understood the basic elements of the story. Evidence of the children's understanding will be provided through the questions you ask and the cartoon strip itself. While the children are working, go round asking questions. Here are some possible questions to check understanding:

– *Who's this? (name of character)*
– *How are the characters related?*
– *What are they doing?*
– *Why is X happy/sad/angry, etc?*

If a child seems to have misunderstood the main ideas of the book, but has enjoyed reading it, show that you are pleased he/she enjoyed it. Remember extensive reading should be done for pleasure as well as for learning!

2 Add your comments and notes from your chat with the child to his/her cartoon strip.

PORTFOLIO

1 Their own cartoon strip is something the children will certainly enjoy having in their portfolio.

2 Apart from your notes, the cartoon strip can be accompanied by the children's notes or a paragraph giving some information on the story, how they liked it, and why they chose that story to work on. The children's progress can also be recorded on the Extensive Reading Checklist in their portfolio. (See Chapter 1, page 31.)

4.6 At the zoo

LEVEL

Pre-intermediate

AGE GROUP

10 and above

TIME

10 minutes

DESCRIPTION

The children scan a brochure to find specific information.

LANGUAGE

Names of animals; time; days of the week; months.

SKILLS

Reading: scanning for specific information; writing (optional in Follow-up).

ASSESSMENT CRITERIA

The children should be able to gather specific information from an authentic written text within a given time limit.

MATERIALS

Worksheet 4.6 (see back of book).

PREPARATION

Photocopy Worksheet 4.6 for each child, or you could use leaflets from a local zoo if they are in English and at an appropriate language level.

IN CLASS

1 Give out Worksheet 4.6 or your leaflet to each child.

2 Ask the children to look at their worksheets to find out what they are supposed to be looking for. Then tell them to scan the brochure very quickly to find the information.

3 They have to answer the questions in five minutes. (Although the time you set can be geared to the level of your class.)

4 Collect the worksheets for checking.

FEEDBACK

Ask the children to explain to the class how they found their answers. By listening to the other children's strategies they could learn effective ways of scanning a passage.

FOLLOW-UP

The children write a list of things they would like to do at the zoo.

VARIATION

1 Tell the children to work in groups and write five questions based on the brochure in Worksheet 4.6. Go round checking their questions to make sure they are not too difficult for the level of the class.

2 The children exchange questions with another group and have five minutes to answer the new set of questions.

3 Get the groups to exchange answers. After the groups have answered the questions they give their answers to the group that wrote them. Each group should then check whether the answers they have received are correct.

4 Each group offers feedback to the other group and allocates them a mark.

ASSESSMENT OF OUTCOME

Use a discrete-point marking scheme. Award two points for each correct answer.

5 Writing

Writing in a foreign language is difficult. It presupposes mastery of a number of language areas such as spelling, grammar, and vocabulary, as well as skills like handwriting and punctuation. This is probably why writing is usually not a favourite activity with young learners.

For this reason writing needs to be made creative, communicative, and enjoyable. This is especially important for young children, whose primary motivation for learning English is not passing an exam. They are motivated by interest in the language, what they can do with it, and by how much fun they have in their language class. Although young children's language can be very limited, they can still do interesting and creative writing activities.

Tasks for assessing young children's writing abilities should therefore be based on the same principles as classroom activities. They should represent realistic and authentic situations and generate interest and enjoyment.

The assessment tasks in this chapter reflect some of the writing skills that children are expected to develop, such as copying letters, words, and short sentences, and writing their own sentences and short paragraphs. These tasks are made interesting and meaningful through topics derived from the children's school and home environment. The activities we provide also reflect the interests of this age group (sports, pets, television programmes, friends and family, games, etc.).

It is relatively easy to assess writing because in most cases the writing is done by a large number of children at the same time and does not require any other materials or technology. A piece of paper is often all they need. As a bonus, much of what is produced as part of the assessment is immediately ready for inclusion in the children's portfolio!

5.1 What's missing?

LEVEL	**Beginners**
AGE GROUP	**6 and above**
TIME	**10–15 minutes**
DESCRIPTION	The children write a shopping list with the help of word and picture cues.

LANGUAGE	Vocabulary related to birthday parties: *birthday cake, burgers, crisps, doughnuts, jelly, biscuits, sandwiches, balloons, party hats, drinks, candles.*
SKILLS	Writing: making a list, copying.
ASSESSMENT CRITERIA	The children should be able to produce legible handwriting, copy a variety of words, and write a shopping list.
MATERIALS	Worksheet 5.1 (see back of book).
PREPARATION	Photocopy Worksheet 5.1 for each child.

IN CLASS

1 Give out Worksheet 5.1. Ask the children to look at the first picture, then at the second one.
2 Explain in the mother tongue that today is their birthday party and everything is ready. Suddenly, they come into the room and find that the cats have ruined the food and party things. What a problem! Now they have to run to the supermarket to replace the missing things.
3 Tell the children to look carefully to see what is missing. They then make a list so that they don't forget anything.
4 Collect the worksheets for checking.

FEEDBACK

1 Ask the children to say what things needed replacing. When they call out a word, write it on the board so that in the end you have the complete list on the board. Accept words similar to the originals, e.g. *drinks* or *orange juice.*
2 The feedback process may end here or, if you haven't collected the papers, ask the children to look at the board and check their answers by using a ✔ next to each correct word and a ✗ next to each misspelled word. If they copied the word wrongly, ask them to copy it again next to their wrong version. This gives further practice in copying because they now have to check and copy from the board. If there are any mistakes in their second copying from the board, take that into consideration in your final marking.

FOLLOW-UP 1

Give the children options for making another list, such as five things they would like to have at their birthday party, five favourite animals, or five favourite colours. They then have to write it down with the help of their coursebooks, picture dictionaries, or other word lists. Afterwards they can decorate their list by drawing the items in it.

FOLLOW-UP 2

A guessing game. Children come to the front of the class holding their list and the others try to find out what is on the list. To make the game more challenging, only allow a limited number of guesses.

VARIATION 1	If the children cannot yet recognize the vocabulary items in this task, you can adapt the worksheet. Delete the word box and write the words under the relevant items. The task will then be assessing copying skills, even if the vocabulary items are new to the children.
VARIATION 2	The worksheet includes all the words the children need. If your class is a little more advanced, partially delete the words. This means that the children have to write and not copy the list. As the words are only partially deleted, this can be a halfway stage between copying and writing, and can be used to test spelling. If the children are even more advanced, you could delete the word list completely, so the children have to rely on their knowledge for the spelling of the words.
VARIATION 3	If you have a mixed-ability class, you can use all the above variations at the same time. Prepare the worksheet in four different versions and give each one to the group who can manage that worksheet level. If you do this, you can assess the whole class with the same task and the same worksheet, but each child will be assessed at his/her own level.
ASSESSMENT OF OUTCOME	Use a discrete-point marking scheme. There are eight missing items: *birthday cake*, *candles*, *drinks*, *balloons*, *party hats*, *jelly*, *burgers*, *sandwiches*. Give each correctly copied word one point and two for legible handwriting.

5.2 Introduce yourself

LEVEL	**Beginners**
AGE GROUP	**6 and above**
TIME	**10 minutes**
DESCRIPTION	The children complete speech bubbles in a cartoon strip.
LANGUAGE	Useful expressions: *My name's ___, I'm ___ years old, I live in ___*, etc.
SKILLS	Writing: simple sentences.
ASSESSMENT CRITERIA	The children should be able to write simple sentences about themselves and produce legible handwriting.
MATERIALS	Worksheet 5.2 (see back of book).
PREPARATION	Photocopy Worksheet 5.2 for each child.

IN CLASS	1 Give out Worksheet 5.2. Ask the children to look at the characters.
	2 Tell them that the two characters have just met for the first time.
	3 The children have to fill in the bubbles to complete the conversation. They are free to choose names for the characters or they can give one of them their own name.
	4 Collect the worksheets for checking.

IN CLASS

1 Give out Worksheet 5.2. Ask the children to look at the characters.
2 Tell them that the two characters have just met for the first time.
3 The children have to fill in the bubbles to complete the conversation. They are free to choose names for the characters or they can give one of them their own name.
4 Collect the worksheets for checking.

FEEDBACK

1 Ask the children to say what they have written and write the expressions on the board.
2 Point out that there are several ways of giving certain information: *I am/I'm seven* or *I am/I'm seven years old*.

FOLLOW-UP

The children work in pairs to role play the dialogue. Put the complete dialogue on the board to help them.

VARIATION 1

If the children are not able to do this task entirely unaided, help them by drawing lines to show the number of words missing, or by writing the first letter of each missing word.

VARIATION 2

For elementary level children, you can add to the cartoon strip and assess expressions like *I like sports* and *I've got two brothers*, etc.

ASSESSMENT OF OUTCOME

1 Use a discrete-point marking scheme. Give the children points for conveying their intended message successfully. They get two and a half points for each communicatively successful expression and two and a half points for handwriting. Ignore minor spelling mistakes which do not interfere with meaning.
2 Alternatively, you can use the writing task marking scheme in 10.10, 'Writing Task Report'.

5.3 My favourite programme

LEVEL

Elementary

AGE GROUP

8 and above

TIME

15–20 minutes

DESCRIPTION

The children write a short paragraph about their favourite television programme with the help of guide questions.

LANGUAGE

Television vocabulary: *comedy, soap opera, love story, news, cartoons,* etc.

SKILLS

Writing: guided writing.

ASSESSMENT CRITERIA

The children should be able to write a short paragraph about their favourite television programme.

MATERIALS

Worksheet 5.3 (see below); paper.

PREPARATION

Photocopy Worksheet 5.3 for each child.

IN CLASS

1   Give out Worksheet 5.3.

Worksheet 5.3

My favourite programme

Name _____ Class _____ Date _____

1   What's your favourite TV programme?
2   What kind of programme is it?
3   What's it about?
4   What day of the week is it on?
5   What time is it on?
6   Who's your favourite character?

My favourite programme

_____

_____

_____

_____

_____

_____

_____

_____

_____

2 Tell the children that by answering the questions in full sentences they will be writing a short paragraph about their favourite television programme.

3 Let them know that they can ask you for help if they do not understand something in the guide questions.

4 If they finish early, they can draw a picture illustrating the programme.

FEEDBACK

1 The children exchange paragraphs with their partners. They read their partner's paragraph and fill in the following form:

My friend's favourite television programme

Name _____   Class _____   Date _____

My partner is _____

1 What is your partner's favourite programme? _____

2 Do you like it? _____

3 Will you watch it? _____

4 When is it on? _____

5 I answered all these questions very easily/easily/not so easily

6 My partner's paragraph is: Very good/Good/OK.

Photocopiable © Oxford University Press

2 Explain to the children that if they answered easily about their partner's writing, it means that their partner did a good job. If not, they should tell their partner later why it wasn't easy to answer the questions. Was it the handwriting, the spelling, or the overall state of the piece?

FOLLOW-UP 1

The children can write a sentence or add speech bubbles to the picture they have drawn (see In Class step 4).

FOLLOW-UP 2

The children imagine they have their own television station and plan a day's programmes.

VARIATION

Instead of a television programme, you can do the same with a radio programme or a film. You can also vary the questions depending on the children's level.

ASSESSMENT OF OUTCOME

1 10.10, 'Writing task report'.

2 Alternatively, use the peer-assessment forms. Collect them and add your comments.

PORTFOLIO

The children can include the tasks along with their reports, the peer-assessment forms, and your comments in their portfolio. They may also want to include material on their favourite programmes, such as pictures, reviews, etc. or their plans from Follow-up 2 if they did it.

5.4 Lost and found

LEVEL

Elementary

AGE GROUP

8 and above

TIME

20 minutes

DESCRIPTION

The children write a description of an object.

LANGUAGE

Vocabulary: colours, shapes, and classroom objects.

SKILLS

Writing: describing objects; listening and speaking (optional).

ASSESSMENT CRITERIA

The children should be able to write a descriptive paragraph.

MATERIALS

Worksheet 5.4 (below); a small piece of paper for each child.

PREPARATION

Photocopy Worksheet 5.4. or draw the worksheet on the board for the children to copy.

Worksheet 5.4

Lost and found
Name _____ Class _____ Date _____
LOST!
More information
1 _____
2 _____
3 _____
4 _____

IN CLASS

1 Get the children to draw something they usually bring to class. Most of the characteristics of any object, such as colour, shape, etc. can be drawn quite easily. If there are any they cannot draw, get them to write them down in note form in the appropriate space on the worksheet, for example *made of* _____, *old/new*, etc. Help the children to add the information.

2 When they have finished, collect the drawings and then redistribute them.

3 Give each child a drawing other than his/her own. Tell the children they have lost this object.

4 They have to write a note with a description of the lost item to put on the 'Lost and Found' notice board. The description should correspond to the drawing they were given as much as possible. You can expect descriptions like the following:

Lost!
A square yellow-and-green rubber.

Pia Maria

Lost!
A small, round yellow purse. It's made of plastic. It has a dog on it.

Jane

Lost!
A long, white ruler. It's old and dirty.

Michael

FEEDBACK

The children take turns to read their descriptions to the class. The others listen to see if the description matches the picture they have drawn. The one whose picture it is stands up.

FOLLOW-UP

Pre-intermediate children can role play 'At the lost and found office'. They play the role of the person working at the office or the person looking for something. They can use the following as a guide:

A *Excuse me, I've lost my pencil case.*
B *Well, we have lots of pencil cases here. What does your case look like?*
A *Mmm, it's plastic and it has a zipper.*

VARIATION 1

The same activity can be carried out with different vocabulary items such as clothes, toys etc.

You can simplify the task by cutting out the 'More information' line and limiting the description to the most basic characteristics of the object.

VARIATION 2

If you want the children to use specific expressions such as *made of* ____, *made in* ____, *old/new*, etc. add them to the worksheet under 'More information'.

ASSESSMENT OF OUTCOME

When you collect the notices use 10.10, 'Writing task report'.

5.5 Pet needs home

LEVEL

Elementary

AGE GROUP

8 and above

TIME

15–20 minutes

DESCRIPTION

The children write an advert describing a pet they want to find a home for.

LANGUAGE

Vocabulary related to pets.

SKILLS

Writing: writing a short paragraph.

ASSESSMENT CRITERIA

The children should be able to write a short paragraph describing an animal.

MATERIALS

Paper or card; an enlarged copy of the advert below, or overhead projector.

He needs a home!

His name is Fluffy.
He's just three months old.
He likes playing with wool.
He likes sleeping, too.

Little Fluffy needs a home.
He's very friendly.

Call Terry on 618-0754325 any time.

PREPARATION	1 Prepare an enlarged photocopy of the advert.
	2 Set up the overhead projector if you are using one.
	3 Tell the children to bring photos of pets or a favourite animal if they have any (for the Variation).
IN CLASS	1 Put the enlarged advert about a pet looking for a home up on the board or on the overhead projector.
	2 Discuss the advert with the children, for example, *What is this advert for? When can we phone?*
	3 Tell the children that they have a pet (a puppy or kitten) which they are not allowed to keep, so they want to find it a home. They are going to write an advert to post around the neigbourhood.
	4 Give out a piece of paper to each child. The children write the advert. Go round monitoring as they write and offer help when needed.
	5 Fast finishers can draw a picture of their pet.
FEEDBACK	1 Peer-feedback. The children exchange adverts with their partners.
	2 Write questions on the board for example:
	– *Did you like the advert?*
	– *Was it easy to understand?*
	– *Would you take this pet home?*
	– *Why? Why not?*
	3 Ask the children to read each others' adverts, answer these questions, and discuss their work, in their mother tongue if necessary.
	4 You can also decide on the questions after discussing with them what makes a good advert.
FOLLOW-UP	1 Discuss with the children what responsibilities are involved when one has a pet.
	2 The children write a list of things they will do for the pet:
	– *I will take it for a walk every day.*
	– *I will play with it/feed it, etc.*
VARIATION	The children can write about real or imaginary pets. Some children, for example, love having unusual animals such as snakes, lizards, geckos, praying mantes, etc.
ASSESSMENT OF OUTCOME	Use 10.10, 'Writing task report', and peer-assessment.
PORTFOLIO	The children can include the advert in their portfolio.

5.6 Writing about people

LEVEL	**Pre-intermediate**
AGE GROUP	**10 and above**
TIME	**20–25 minutes**
DESCRIPTION	The children write questions and a description of a person.
LANGUAGE	Vocabulary for descriptions: professions; *was born in*; *intelligent, generous, smart, kind, witty, interesting,* etc.
SKILLS	Writing: question formation, and giving biographical information and personality traits.
ASSESSMENT CRITERIA	The children should be able to write questions to elicit biographical information and personality traits, and write a short description of a person with the help of guide questions.
MATERIALS	Photographs of a friend or relative.
PREPARATION	Ask the children to bring a picture of a friend or relative, preferably someone unknown to the rest of the class.

IN CLASS

1 Show the children a picture of a friend or relative of yours. Encourage them to ask questions about him/her.

2 The children exchange their pictures with their partners.

3 The children write five questions on things they want to know about the person in the picture.

4 They give the photograph back to the owner together with their questions.

5 Each child writes a short paragraph answering their partner's questions about the person in the picture, and shows it to their partner.

FEEDBACK	The children get feedback from discussing the results of their peers' assessment (see Assessment of Outcome below).
FOLLOW-UP	Put the pictures up on the board and give each child a description, making sure he/she hasn't seen it before. Each child reads the passage and then puts it up next to the person it describes.
VARIATION	Instead of a photograph of a real person, the children can draw a monster or a funny figure, and make up biographical data and personality traits.

ASSESSMENT OF OUTCOME

1 Use peer-assessment. Each child completes the assessment form below about his/her partner. The form can be written in the mother tongue if necessary.

Writing about people: peer assessment

Name _____

Partner _____ **Date** _____

1 Did your partner's paragraph answer all your questions?   Yes / No

2 Was it easy to find the answers?   Yes / No

3 Was it easy to understand the paragraph?   Yes / No

4 How would you describe your partner's paragraph?

Very good ☐   Good ☐   OK ☐

Photocopiable © Oxford University Press

2 A first draft may be considered adequate but peer-assessment can also be used as feedback to improve a second draft. In this case, you can either mark the second draft with the same form, completed by the same or another child, or you can mark it using 10.10, 'Writing task report'.

6 Integrated skills

Throughout this book we have argued that assessment should be motivating to children and that one way to achieve this is to make it meaningful and contextualized. This implies integration of skills, as in real life.

Integrating skills can be motivating for young learners because the various skills complement each other and allow children to express more of themselves, something they are not always able to do when using only one skill. Although children may have limited competence in the four skills, this should not prevent them from putting the little knowledge they have to real communicative use. For example, if we accept that writing follows speaking, listening, and reading, we should seize any opportunity for children to exercise their limited competence in writing. Writing is less threatening and more natural to children if it is contextualized and regarded as an extension of the other skills. By integrating the skills we can present whole communication contexts to the children.

In any assessment activity that includes more than one skill, the children will show their competence in each individual skill by achieving the specific aim for that particular skill such as writing a script. In addition, children will also show their ability to use all the skills to achieve the overall aim of the activity such as putting on a play. You may want to assess all the skills involved, or focus on certain skills only.

The children's specific language skills can be measured by using the Assessment of Outcome sections.

6.1 Endangered species

LEVEL	**Beginners**
AGE GROUP	**6 and above**
TIME	**3 x 40-minute lessons (minimum)**
OVERALL DESCRIPTION	The children learn about endangered species and make an oral presentation with the help of stick puppets.
OVERALL LANGUAGE	Names of animals and their food preferences (plants, fish, etc.); colours.

SKILLS

Speaking: oral presentation.
Listening: listening for specific information.
Reading: reading for details and following instructions.
Writing: copying.

ASSESSMENT CRITERIA

The children should be able to copy individual words, match words with pictures, match paragraphs with pictures, follow written instructions to make a puppet, make a very simple oral presentation, listen to an oral presentation, and find specific information.

MATERIALS

Worksheets 6.1a and c (see back of book); pictures of the animals you are assessing; A4 paper for each child; sticky tape; popsicle/lollipop sticks or pencils; scissors; coloured pencils. Optional: magazines; books; leaflets; Internet websites (printed out or bookmarked in your computer); camera; cassette-recorder; camcorder; overhead projector.

PREPARATION

1 Photocopy Worksheet 6.1b on page 82 (optional). Photocopy and cut up Worksheets 6.1.a and c for each child.

2 Ask the children to bring in any illustrations or toys or books they can find of the following animals: *whale, panda, rhino, tiger, crocodile, koala bear, polar bear, gorilla.*

3 If possible, choose one of the animals and make your own stick puppet as a model for the children.

4 Set up the overhead projector if you are using one.

1 Colour the bear.

2 Cut out the bear. ✂

3 Stick the bear on your pencil.

Lesson 1

The children should be able to copy individual words and match words with pictures.

IN CLASS

1   Introduce the topic to the children by talking about endangered species. Show pictures, and write the names of the animals and other relevant vocabulary on the board (for example, *bamboo*) and get the children to practise saying the names.

2   Give out Worksheet 6.1b or a similar chart and ask the children to draw the animals and copy the animals' names from the board. Alternatively ask the children to copy Worksheet 6.1a from the board, or just to draw the pictures.

Worksheet 6.1b

A			
Name	Name	Name	Name
B			
Name	Name	Name	Name

Photocopiable © Oxford University Press

3   Divide the class into groups of four. If you have a mixed-ability class, make sure to include children from all levels of ability in each group.

4   Assign four animals (set A or set B) to each group. Ask the children to each choose a different animal from their group's set and find a picture or other information about it to bring to class for the next lesson. They can begin their search in class if you have a selection of magazines, books, leaflets, or access to the Internet. Or they can search at home with the help of parents or other family members. Make sure each member of a group chooses a different animal.

FEEDBACK

1   Go round looking at the children's work and offering them feedback.

2   Put the completed charts on the notice board and invite the children to view each other's work.

Lesson 2

ASSESSMENT
CRITERIA

The children should be able to match paragraphs with pictures, follow written instructions, and make a puppet.

IN CLASS

1   Revise the animals the children learnt about in their previous lesson and invite them to show the class the pictures they found. If they have information to share with the class, either allow them to use the mother tongue or help them by giving them the necessary vocabulary and expressions.

2   The pictures can later be displayed on the notice board. If any of the children are interested, they could take some of their material home and prepare posters to put on the notice board. Help them with ideas.

3   Put the children in the same groups they were in for Lesson 1.

4   Give out Worksheet 6.1a, according to which set of animals the children are working with.

5   Tell the groups to match the paragraphs with the pictures and fill in the names of the animals.

6   Next, tell the children they are going to make puppets. Each child chooses one of their group's four animals for their puppet.

7   Put the instructions for making the puppet on the board (see page 81). Tell the children to cut out the picture of their animal and follow the instructions for making their puppet. If you have made a model, put it where the children can see it. The puppets can be finished at home if there is not enough time in class.

FEEDBACK

1   While the children are working on their puppets, go round the groups asking them to take out Worksheet 6.1a again. Read the passages through with them and check their answers.

2   The children can also mark themselves out of 20, allocating five points for each correct match. You can then check their marking and add comments.

Lesson 3

**ASSESSMENT
CRITERIA**

The children should be able to give a very simple oral presentation, listen to an oral presentation, and extract specific information.

IN CLASS

1   The children sit in their groups. If any of them have brought posters to class, allow time for them to show their posters and display them on the notice board.

2   Get all the children to show their puppets to the class.

3   Explain that they are going to look at the reading passages on Worksheet 6.1a again and that each of them is going to give a short oral presentation of the animal they made a puppet of.

4   Allow time for the children to read their chosen passage and think about what they are going to say.

5   The children can practise their presentation with a partner in their group, taking turns to listen and help their partner to prepare.

6   Go round the groups making sure all the children are doing their preparation. Offer help when needed.

7   Invite the children to give their oral presentations. The children hold up the puppet of their animal while giving it. Shy or weak children may choose not to give a presentation, in which case make sure that their animals are presented by someone in another group.

8   Hand out Worksheet 6.1c and give each group the part about the animals they *haven't* worked on already. Explain that while the children presenting the animals in set A are speaking, the children who worked with set B listen to the presentations and circle any words they hear on Worksheet 6.1c. If you have more than one child presenting each animal, the children will have the opportunity of hearing about it several times. If not, the class may ask a child to repeat his/her presentation.

FEEDBACK

1   Speaking: oral presentation. If the children are willing, you could record their presentations on cassettes. Each child can listen to the recording either at home or at a time scheduled with you. You can then discuss the performance together.

2   If the presentations are not recorded, take notes and discuss the presentation with each child. Comment on it privately soon afterwards, while it is fresh in both your minds.

3   Listening: write the answers to the word-circling activity on the board so that the children can check their answers.

4   Tell the children that they get one point for every correct word they circled. They can add up their marks themselves. Check their marks later and add your comments.

FOLLOW-UP 1

The children have prepared a lot of material during this project (drawings, posters, puppets). This material can be displayed. Help the children to prepare suitable headings and put the display up in an obvious place in your school.

FOLLOW-UP 2

If the children would like to, let them visit another class to give their presentations. You or the class teacher can present them. The host class may even like to do the listening comprehension activity on Worksheet 6.1c as they listen to your class.

FOLLOW-UP 3

If they are interested in animals, the children might like to join an environmental organization such as the World Wildlife Fund (WWF). Help them to fill in the forms if they want to join. Encourage them to find out more by checking websites such as:

World Wildlife Fund http://www.worldwildlife.org
The International Rhino Foundation http://www.rhinos-irf.org
Endangered Wildlife Trust http://www.ewt.org.za/
The Dian Fossey Gorilla Fund International
http://www.informatics.org/gorilla
Wildlife Conservation Network http://www.wildnet.org

VARIATION

If you don't have enough time to carry out this project with your class, consider leaving out a step or assigning some of the tasks for homework and involving the parents. If, for example, the chart you handed out at the beginning has the names of the animals already written on it, the drawing and colouring of the animals can be done at home.

ASSESSMENT OF OUTCOME

1 To get an overall picture of the children's performance you need to look at all the work produced throughout this project. You can do this bit by bit or collect all the work together when the children are preparing their portfolio package.

2 You can look at the assessment criteria for each stage/lesson and make sure that you assess the aims that are relevant to you. If, for example, copying is too basic an aim for your class, you can leave out that step and concentrate on the more demanding aims of the oral presentation and the listening activity.

3 The outcomes can be assessed in the following way:

Lesson 1
Allocate 20 points to the end product of this stage. Break down the points in the following way:

Give eight points for copying correctly, one for each word.
Give eight points for matching correctly, one for each word.
Give four points for overall quality of handwriting.

Lesson 2
1 Allocate 20 points to the reading activity, five points for each correct paragraph match.

2 Successfully executed puppets show that the children followed the instructions. Nevertheless, it is very informative to observe the children and keep notes on how they worked during this stage. For example, did the child wait and copy other children's actions, or did he/she seem to be confident and understand the instructions?

Lesson 3
1 Oral presentation: Use self-assessment for this (see 8.8) and discuss the results with the child. You could also observe the presentation and assess it using 10.9a, 'Speaking task report'.

You may only be able to do this for a few children unless you are recording the presentations.

2   Listening: Allocate one point for each correct word.

PORTFOLIO

1   The children should all have a big selection of material by the end of this project. Help them to staple everything together and make a card cover. Encourage them to add comments on their work. The comments can be either in the mother tongue or in English, if you help them.

2   If a child has prepared extra material because of a particular interest in the topic, include that in the portfolio as well.

3   If you have been taking photos during the presentations or other stages of the project, the children could choose which ones they want to include. They and you can also add comments to accompany the photos.

4   Finally, your comments on the child's work and any reports you may have compiled can also be part of the package the children include in their portfolio.

6.2   A mini-play

LEVEL

Elementary and above

AGE GROUP

8 and above

TIME

Lesson 1: 40 minutes
Lessons 2 and 3: 2 x 20 minutes
Lesson 4: 30 minutes + to present the play

OVERALL DESCRIPTION

The children work in groups to prepare a mini-play.

OVERALL LANGUAGE

Depends on the story used.

OVERALL SKILLS

Speaking: expressing feelings with appropriate intonation and expression.
Reading: comprehending extensive texts.
Writing: writing a script.

OVERALL ASSESSMENT CRITERIA

The children should be able to comprehend an extensive written text, write a basic/simple script with the help of written or visual information, read a passage or a part in a script, projecting the appropriate feelings (interpretative reading), perform a part in a short play, work as a group, and co-operate successfully.

MATERIALS

Story-books or class readers; cards; markers; (optional) cassettes and recorders; camcorder; camera

PREPARATION

1 This assessment is based on stories or readers the children have previously read and perhaps worked with on book reports. The whole class might work on the same book, but on different scenes. Otherwise, the class can work with a selection of different readers.

2 When the children have prepared and written up their scripts, photocopy each script for each member of the group.

Lesson 1

ASSESSMENT CRITERIA

The children should be able to comprehend an extensive written text, write a basic/simple script with the help of written or visual information, work as a group, and co-operate successfully.

IN CLASS

1 Explain to the children that they are going to work on one of the stories or readers they have read to prepare a mini-play.

2 Divide the children into groups of four (or six if you have a large class). If the children are working on a selection of books, set up the groups according to the book they want to work on. If the class works on one reader with a long story, first discuss whether it can be divided into various scenes.

3 Once the class agrees on the scenes, write them clearly on the board. Put the children into groups according to the scene or story they want to work on. (This may also dictate how many children can join a particular group, and you may have to add or remove characters.)

4 To ensure that all the children contribute to the script writing, ask the groups to assign roles before they begin. Then during the script writing, make each child responsible for writing his/her character's part. Go round checking the roles are within each child's abilities. If you need more roles, add a character to 'echo' another, for example, in *April Fool's Day* another character can echo Mr Nosey. This sort of role is particularly suitable for weaker learners.

5 Tell the groups to start working on the script. The following example is based on the Graded Reader *Pat and her Picture*, by Rosemary Border, Oxford University Press.

6 Go round monitoring the groups and offering help when needed, encouraging the children or giving them ideas to get them started. Check that the children are not writing very long scripts. Remember that they also need time to perform them!

7 When they have finished and after your feedback, ask the children to decide who will write out or type up the script. The child in charge should bring you the script before the beginning of the next lesson, so that you can photocopy it for all the children in the group. If photocopying is a problem, allocate time either in this lesson or the next for all the children to write up the script neatly.

Sample story script 1

Scene 1	
Bus driver	Hello, Pat! Hello, Jim! Sit down, please!
Pat	Yes, Mr. Brown!
Jim	OK, Mr. Brown!
Scene 2	
Jim	Hello, what's your name?
Pat	Pat!
Scene 3	
Miss White	Hello, children! How are you?
Pat and Jim	Fine, thanks!
Miss White	What's this, Pat?
Pat	It's my picture, Miss White. It's a bus driver.
Miss White	He's got a gold tooth. It's Mr. Brown.
Scene 4	
Bus driver	Who's this, Pat? He's got a gold tooth. Is it me?
Pat	Yes, Mr. Brown.
Bus driver	Thank you, Pat. I like it.

Sample story script 2 (one scene only)
This example is based on the reader *April Fool's Day* by
L. G. Alexander, Longman.

Narrator	This is Puddleton, a small village. It's morning. It's 6 o'clock. Everyone's sleeping. Only Joe Selby is working in his garden. Today is April 1st, April Fool's Day. Joe wants to play a joke on a friend.
[Joe is digging in his garden]	
Nosey	Good morning, Joe. Are you busy?
Joe	Good morning, Nosey. Yes, I'm very busy.
Nosey	What are you doing?
Joe	I'm digging a hole.
Nosey	Why?
Joe	I'm looking for oil. Don't tell your friends!
Nosey	I promise.
Joe	I'm going to be a rich man.
Nosey	I must go to work now. Goodbye.
Joe	Goodbye.

FEEDBACK

1 Working and co-operating in a group: observe the groups during the lesson and take notes on how they work together. Later, towards the end of the lesson, spend time with each group and discuss how well they worked together as a group and how efficient they were in preparing their script.

2 Comprehending extensive texts and writing a script: try to read the scripts or sections of the scripts the groups are working on. If you see anything that indicates lack of understanding of the reader, talk to the children. Question them and challenge them to explain, so that you get an insight into their understanding of the reader.

3 Comment on their use of the dialogue format, vocabulary, and expression.

Lesson 2

ASSESSMENT CRITERIA

The children should be able to read a passage or a part in a script, projecting the appropriate feelings (interpretative reading), work as a group, and co-operate successfully.

IN CLASS

1 Give out the photocopies of the scripts. Each group gets the script they prepared in the previous lesson.

2 Give the groups time to go over their script silently so that they remember their parts and the play as a whole.

3 Tell them to rehearse the play. They should read it out loud at least three or four times. This will give you time to listen to a number of groups. Also suggest that they record themselves on cassette and use the recording to help them. They can listen to themselves either in class or at home and spot any mistakes they might be making, either in their use of the language or in their interpretation of the script.

4 When they feel ready, they can decide what props they will need for the play. Make sure they don't plan over-ambitious props. If you have examples from other mini-plays, show them some sample props. Go round the classroom monitoring their decisions on props.

5 For scene-setting, one idea is to draw or write the names of the places where the scenes take place, for example, 'The school', 'The school bus' on cards. One child can then hold up the cards and walk across the stage announcing the changes of scene before the actors appear. *Pat and her Picture*, for example, would need only two cards, with words or a picture, or both: 'On the bus' (Scenes 1, 2, and 4), and 'At school' (Scene 3). The example scene from *April Fool's Day* again only needs two cards: 'Puddleton village', and 'Joe's garden'.

6 Once they have decided on the props they need, they can either prepare them in class or work on them at home.

7 The children have to try and learn their parts by heart. This can also be done at home with the help of parents, older siblings, or other family or friends.

FEEDBACK

1 Props: Monitor the children's work and offer feedback on the props.

2 Interpretative reading: listen to the groups while they are rehearsing and offer feedback on their interpretation of the script.

3 If the children have recorded themselves, you might get the group to play back the recording and discuss with you the highlights of the play as well as areas in need of improvement.

Lesson 3

ASSESSMENT CRITERIA

The children should be able to perform a part in a short play, work as a group, and co-operate successfully.

IN CLASS

1 Allow the children time to get into their groups and check their props.

2 If they are happy with the props, they can have a full rehearsal of the play with actions, etc. If you have a small number of children in the class, they can work in different corners of the classroom. If your class is of average size and the school has public areas (library, garden, lobby etc.), you could probably get permission to use those. Set a time limit for the children. If you have a very large class, you might want to break this stage up into different lessons, during which different groups rehearse while the rest of the class works on other activities.

3 Monitor thc rehearsals and remind the children that their play should not be too long.

FEEDBACK

Co-operation and performing in a play: give the group feedback on the quality of their performance as a whole.

Lesson 4

ASSESSMENT CRITERIA

The childrcn should be able to perform a part in a short play, work as a group, and co-operate successfully.

IN CLASS

1 The groups present their plays in class. This can take place over several lessons so that each group can present their play. Another way of presenting the plays is to invite the children and their families and friends to a weekend session when your groups present their plays. If your class has worked on different scenes of the same book, put the performance together so that the audience sees the whole story scene by scene.

2 If possible video and/or take photographs of the children. If the parents are invited you can get some help from them, too!

FEEDBACK

The class or group completes a peer-assessment form for each group (see the next page).

Peer-assessment form for mini-play

Name _____ Date _____			
Assessment of group _____			
The play was based on the reader _____			
I liked watching the play.	😊	😐	☹️
I liked the props.	😊	😐	☹️
The children in the group are good actors.	😊	😐	☹️
The story was interesting.	😊	😐	☹️
The story was the same as in the book.	😊	😐	☹️
The actors spoke clearly.	😊	😐	☹️

Photocopiable © Oxford University Press

FOLLOW-UP

1 If the children took photos while they were performing, the most interesting photos can be displayed. The children write captions or speech bubbles for each photo and put them up on the notice board. You could turn this into a competition and give a prize for the funniest caption.

2 If the plays are performed in public, the groups can prepare posters announcing and advertising the performances. The posters can then be placed around the school.

VARIATION 1

If you are working with an advanced class and one reader, you could have groups working on various scenes and put all the scenes together for an end-of-year performance.

VARIATION 2

Instead of writing a script following a scene or the plot of a reader, the children could write their own scene or change a scene, for example, by changing the characters' personalities or changing the ending.

ASSESSMENT OF OUTCOME

1 Comprehending extensive written texts: when you assess the scripts prepared by the children and take into account the discussions you had with them about the script (especially if there were any misunderstandings), you get a good picture of the children's abilities to comprehend an extensive written text appropriate to their level. Your notes on their comprehension should accompany the scripts when they are entered in the children's portfolios.

2 Writing a simple script with the help of written or visual information. Assess their writing using 10.10, 'Writing task report'.

3 Reading a passage or a part in a script, projecting the appropriate feelings (interpretative reading): if you made a video or audio recording it provides a permanent record of the children's achievement of this aim. Alternatively, you can use observation notes.

4 Performing a part in a short play: the peer-assessment forms can be discussed with them.

5 Working as a group and co-operating successfully: use your notes and the group work assessment form in the Introduction, page 18.

6 The children's performance, their interpretive reading, their group work, and their co-operation skills can be discussed with the group if there is time. They could watch and discuss the video if one was made. If you feel that your class is able to handle a public discussion of each group, you might try showing the video to the whole class and discussing the above issues openly. Only do this if you are sure all the children are very supportive. But the fact that all the children are being treated in the same way should make them considerate towards their classmates. Encourage them to offer positive assessment and constructive comments.

7 Finally, all these assessment instruments should go in the children's portfolio to give a complete picture of their performance in this task.

PORTFOLIO

1 A selection of the captions and pictures prepared by the children can be included in their portfolios. You may also arrange for copies of the tape or video to be included in each child's portfolio if you recorded the plays. The tapes can be accompanied by the children's comments on the activity.

2 Add reports, observation comments, and other notes that you might have made in assessing this task.

6.3 Favourite songs and musicians

LEVEL

Pre-intermediate

AGE GROUP

10 and above

TIME

Lesson 1 and Lesson 2: 40 minutes each
Lesson 3: 20 minutes +
Lesson 4: 20 minutes for each group to present their work.
(Presentations can take place over a series of lessons.)

OVERALL DESCRIPTION

Children work in groups to prepare a presentation about their favourite musicians.

OVERALL LANGUAGE

Zodiac signs, birthdays, nationalities, hobbies, dates, and other information about famous people. Agreeing, disagreeing, making suggestions: *Let's _____; Why don't we _____?*

OVERALL SKILLS

Reading: Comprehending extensive texts; searching for information from a variety of authentic sources.
Writing: Making a poster; writing a paragraph about a famous person.
Speaking: Discussing (agreeing, disagreeing, making suggestions, expressing opinions); giving an oral presentation.
Listening: Listening to authentic texts (songs); intensive listening

OVERALL ASSESSMENT CRITERIA

The children should be able to comprehend extensive texts, search for information from a variety of authentic sources; co-operate well with other children in their group, orally make suggestions/agree/disagree/express an opinion; write a paragraph about a famous person, make a poster; write questions about a famous person; make a short oral presentation; extract details from a listening text.

MATERIALS

Sources of information about musicians, for example, magazines, newspapers, books, websites; camera and film (if you want to take photos); video camera (if you want to video the presentations); markers, crayons, scissors, glue and large pieces of card (for the poster); CD player or audio cassette player.

PREPARATION

Ask children to bring their own information to class (see above).

Lesson 1

ASSESSMENT CRITERIA

The children should be able to co-operate well with other children in their group, orally make suggestions/agree/disagree /express an opinion, comprehend extensive texts, and search for information from a variety of authentic sources.

IN CLASS

1 Ask the children if they have any favourite songs, who they are by, and finally, who their favourite musicians are. Write their favourite musicians on the board.

2 Ask them to prepare an oral presentation about their favourite musicians so as to introduce their classmates and you to the music they like.

3 Divide children into groups of 4 according to their musical preferences. Try not to have two groups dealing with the same musicians.

4 Children discuss in their groups what information they should include in their presentation. Remind them that they should try and use English as much as possible. Write on the board some of the phrases that they will most likely need, for example:
   – *Let's …*
   – *Why don't we ..?*
   – *Yes, it's a good idea.*
   – *I agree.*
   – *I don't agree.*
   – *I think we should …*

5 Encourage them to keep notes on what they decide.

6 Monitor the groups to try to make sure they speak in English.

7 Once they agree on the information they will be looking for, the groups discuss where and how they are going to work, what sources they are going to use, and who is going to do what (for example, research should be shared among group members depending on the sources each child has access to).

8 They also decide on a song they can play to the class.

9 If there is time they can start their search using the materials brought in. If there isn't enough time, the materials can be left in class or, perhaps, borrowed by children who have no access to target-language material at home.

FEEDBACK

Procedure and co-operation Join the groups towards the end of their assigned time and check that they have organized their searching tasks appropriately and arranged times and places to meet if necessary. Offer feedback on how they worked as a group.

Speaking Use Worksheet 8.8 (page 121). You can add categories such as *I made a lot of suggestions*, if necessary, or you may change categories, for example, *I asked a lot of questions* to *I agreed/I disagreed with my friends' suggestions*. Collect the forms and offer the children feedback, from your observations, on how well they did during the task.

In a class discussion, ask the children to report back on what information they agreed to include in their presentations. Write this on the board, creating a checklist for all the groups. For example:

Name, Real name, Age, Birthday, Zodiac Sign, Country they live in, Nationality, Hobbies, Hits, Girlfriend/Boyfriend, Other information.

Reading Ask individual children questions while they are working, such as *Are you finding this difficult? Are there many difficult words?*

How do you deal with the words you don't know? This information will help you to give useful feedback.

Lesson 2

ASSESSMENT CRITERIA

The children should be able to: co-operate well with other children in their group; write a paragraph about a famous person ; make a poster; write questions about a famous person.

IN CLASS

1 The children sit with their groups to pool the information they have gathered. If the group is satisfied with their material, they prepare the text for the oral presentation. Otherwise they continue searching for information within a time-limit set by you. Advise them to prepare a written text first so that they can use it for their rehearsals/preparation.

2 If the children are presenting on a group of musicians (for example, The Beatles), each child can prepare for and present one artist, whereas if they are concentrating on only one artist (such as George Michael) they should break up the presentation into parts based on the checklist created in Lesson 1. This way each child has a specific part to prepare.

3 Encourage children to take turns reading their work to the group to see how it sounds when it is all put together. They should also time themselves and offer each other feedback.

4 Divide the groups into pairs to deal with the poster and the listening activities.

   Poster Children prepare a poster with information about the musician/s and additional visual material which they display on the board.

   Listening activities Based on their presentation, they prepare listening activities such as questions, which they will give to the rest of the class to do during the presentation. The children write up the listening activities in the form of a handout.

5 If children don't have time to finish the poster and the listening activities, they can continue at home or in the next lesson.

FEEDBACK

1 Ask each group to go through their presentation with you and discuss whether they think it provides adequate information about the artist, whether it is well organized, etc.

2 Check how the poster and the listening activities are progressing. Invite the children to contribute ideas and check that they have enough time or whether they are willing to work at home. Make sure that the song they chose is appropriate to be presented in class.

3 Also offer feedback on how the group co-operated and ask the children to tell you how they think their group is working, if they are having any problems, and how they can improve their group work.

Lesson 3

ASSESSMENT
CRITERIA

The children should be able to co-operate well with other children in their group; write a paragraph about a famous person; make a poster; write questions about a famous person.

IN CLASS

1 In their groups, the children check each other's work (make comments, additions, etc). Monitor the groups.

2 Remind them to give you the completed handout with the listening activities/questions so that you can photocopy it in time for their presentation.

3 They rehearse their presentations.

FEEDBACK

Presentation text, poster and listening activities
Offer feedback on their work. You may need to provide guidance for the handout, as sometimes children include difficult questions for their classmates.
Oral presentation Find time during the children's rehearsals to listen in. Remind them to speak loudly, clearly, and not too fast. Tell them that they can use notes but they should be comfortable enough to be able to look at their audience and not simply read from their notes.
Co-operation See feedback for Lesson 2.

Lesson 4

**ASSESSMENT
CRITERIA**

The children should be able to make a short oral presentation and extract details from a listening text.

IN CLASS

1 Allow the group doing the presentation time for one final rehearsal. This may be done while the rest of the class is involved in a silent activity.

2 The group gives out the activities/handout they prepared.

3 The presentation takes place while the rest of the class carries out the listening activities.

4 Encourage the group to ask if their classmates would like them to repeat the presentation.

5 The group plays the song they selected.

6 The group collects the handouts to mark at home and return later.

7 They put the answers to the listening activities on the board.

8 If there is time, the class can ask questions relating to the presentation, or listen to the song again.

FEEDBACK

Peer feedback After each presentation, the class – or a section of the class – fills in assessment/feedback cards (see below). The group doing the presentation collect the cards and study them later during a meeting/conference with you. During this meeting, discuss the points made on the cards and invite self-assessment from the children. Ask them how well they think they did, what were the good points of their presentation, what things went wrong, and what could be improved in the future.

FOLLOW-UP

1 Each group writes up a short written presentation about their chosen musicians. All the presentations can be put together, photocopied and stapled, and given to the class as a booklet. The songs may also be collected and a class cassette can be prepared to accompany the booklet. Children may want to help you with the preparation of a class cassette. Let them do it!

2 The posters and visual material materials can be arranged into a giant poster which can stay in class or be put on display in a public area of the school.

3 You can arrange for your class to visit other classes and do their presentations.

Peer-assessment card for oral presentation

Name: _____	**Date:** _____
Presentation by Group: _____	
Name of Musician / Group: _____	
The group spoke loudly.	Yes / No
The group spoke clearly.	Yes / No
I could understand them.	Yes / No
The presentation was interesting.	Yes / No
The presentation helped me answer all the questions in the handout.	Yes / No
I liked the presentation.	Yes / No
The poster was interesting.	Yes / No
I liked the poster.	Yes / No
Comments:	

VARIATION 1

You can have presentations about the children's favourite actors or important/famous people. In the case of actors, the children can show extracts from films, if you have access to a video and television.

VARIATION 2

If you are short of time many tasks can be carried out at home, especially if children live close to each other.

ASSESSMENT OF OUTCOME

Co-operation
Observe the children during group work. You can also chat/conference with the children (see feedback stages). Make notes on your observations and conferences soon after they take place. Use the group work assessment form (see page 18). You may also add some of the points arising from your observation and conference notes.

Reading
Observe and conference/chat with the children (see feedback in Lesson 1). You should again try to keep notes on the information you collect. These notes may be entered in children's portfolios along with the children's work and comments

Speaking
Speaking may be assessed through one or more of the following:
– self-assessment 8.8
– peer-assessment (see peer-assessment card above)
– observation notes
– Speaking Task Report 10.9b for performance in the discussion task (Lesson 1)
– Speaking Task Report 10.9a for the oral presentation.

Writing
Use the Writing Marking Scheme in 10.10. You can complete a report for each task, or fill in one report based on all the writing tasks the child has carried out.

Listening
The children have prepared listening handouts and they have also taken responsibility for correcting and marking them. Have a look at the completed and marked handouts before they are returned and record each child's achievement.

PORTFOLIO

1 If you videotaped or recorded the presentations, the children may want to include the video or audio cassette in their portfolios. If you take photographs, the children can choose some to go in their portfolios. They can also add captions or speech bubbles to the photos. You can also include a class tape with all the songs presented.

2 Include reports, notes from conferences and observations, and self- and peer-assessment forms for each child.

7 Grammar

This chapter on grammar assessment tasks was not written in the belief that grammar should be taught separately but because teachers need to know their children's level of understanding of grammatical structures. The ultimate goal of teaching grammar is not for children to learn forms and abstract rules but to be able to convey their intended meaning effectively.

Although communication is the primary goal, no one can communicate effectively and appropriately if their use of language is inaccurate. Even though some inaccuracies can be overlooked in foreign learners, especially in children, learners need to be made aware that inaccurate grammar interferes with meaning. It is also desirable to assess grammar separately because it is unfair to penalize grammatical errors when assessing communicative ability in other skills.

A short-term goal for teaching grammar could be to help children understand how language works. This can be especially useful with any language that children are already using as 'chunks'. For example, a child may be using phrases such as *My name is* _____, without being able to manipulate the components and use them in other contexts. When you focus on possessive pronouns, you help children to maximize the potential use of this structure by enabling them to create new sentences such as *His name is* _____, *Her name is* _____.

Focusing on grammatical structures also helps you to get feedback on the way you teach particular structures. Children's errors often lead back to the presentation of a structure in a way that has confused the children. This becomes more obvious when a large number of the children in the class seem to be making the same mistake. Feedback from children can often be very useful, particularly for beginner teachers.

Grammar assessment should be a natural extension of the approach used in class. As stated in the Introduction, encouraging motivation and positive attitudes towards learning and the target language should feature high in our priorities when teaching young learners. This applies equally when we assess grammar.

7.1 Colour the picture

LEVEL	**Beginners**
AGE GROUP	**6 and above**
TIME	**10 minutes**
DESCRIPTION	The children focus on prepositions, colouring objects in a picture by following instructions.
LANGUAGE	Prepositions: *in*, *on*, *under*; colours.
SKILLS	Reading: recognizing and understanding selected prepositions.
ASSESSMENT CRITERIA	The children should be able to understand the meaning of selected prepositions.
MATERIALS	Worksheet 7.1 (see back of book); coloured pencils; overhead projector and coloured markers (optional); paper.

PREPARATION

1 Photocopy Worksheet 7.1 for each child.
2 Set up the overhead projector if you are using one.

IN CLASS

1 Show the class Worksheet 7.1 or put it up on the overhead projector. Tell the children they first have to read the instructions at the bottom of the page. They then follow the instructions and colour the picture.
2 Hand out Worksheet 7.1.
3 The children complete the task.
4 Collect the Worksheets.

FEEDBACK

1 If you have an overhead projector, ask a few children to come out to the front. Give them coloured markers and ask them to colour the picture according to the instructions.
2 Alternatively, you could draw the picture on the board or enlarge the worksheet before you go through the answers with the class.

FOLLOW-UP

1 Hand out a piece of paper to each child for them to draw their own pictures and write simple sentences like the ones on the worksheet.
2 They then exchange papers with their partners and colour each other's pictures.

VARIATION

If the children don't know the colours, put a chart on the board for them to use as a reference.

ASSESSMENT OF OUTCOME

Use a discrete-point marking scheme.

PORTFOLIO	The children can put their pictures in their portfolios if they wish.

7.2 I like – I don't like

LEVEL	**Beginners**
AGE GROUP	**8 and above**
TIME	**20 minutes**
DESCRIPTION	The children play a game focusing on the verb *like*.
LANGUAGE	Affirmative and negative forms of the verb *like* in the present simple tense.
SKILLS	Writing: writing sentences with *like* and *don't like*.
ASSESSMENT CRITERIA	The children should be able to use the verb *like* in the affirmative and negative and to express likes and dislikes.
MATERIALS	Worksheets 7.2a and b (see back of book); dice; word and picture cards below; one record chart for each group (see next page).
PREPARATION	1 Photocopy Worksheet 7.2 or prepare a circle and cards with your own choice of objects or actions. You will need one circle for each group of four children.
	2 Make two sets of picture cards for each group (see below).
	3 Photocopy Worksheet 7.2b (showing likes and dislikes) for each child.
	4 Make a class record chart like the one on the next page.

| rice | eggs | milk | chocolates | salad | pizza |

IN CLASS	1 Divide the class into groups of four and give each group a numbered circle (Worksheet 7.2a) and a die.
	2 Hand out three cards to each child.

3   Explain to the children that their three cards represent things they like. If there is a picture on the circle that they don't have on their cards, it's something they 'don't like'.

4   Tell the children that each of them will throw the die four times. Each time they throw it they fill in their worksheet. If the number on the die corresponds to the number of an object in the circle, and they have the picture, they complete the sentence on the worksheet, for example, *I like milk*. If they don't have the picture corresponding to the number on the die, they fill in the worksheet with, for example, *I don't like pizza*.

5   The aim of this game is to be the first to complete three *I like ___* sentences on the worksheet. If by chance the same number comes up more than once, the children can write either *I really like pizza* or *I really don't like pizza*.

6   Appoint a group secretary to record the children's performance (see Assessment of Outcome below).

7   The children take turns throwing the die until someone wins. You could also continue the game until all the children have completed their worksheets.

FEEDBACK

While you are collecting the record charts (see Assessment of Outcome), comment on the children's performance.

FOLLOW-UP

Ask the children to make true statements about the cards they have. They can do this either orally or in writing.

ASSESSMENT OF OUTCOME

1   Observe the children and take notes.

2   Give the group secretaries a copy of the record chart below. They tick a box each time one of the children forms a correct sentence. At the end the group can look at their results and discuss their performance.

3   Collect the charts and Worksheet 7.2b for your records. You may like to monitor in case the secretaries don't know when sentences are correct or not.

Name	I like … / I don't like	I like … / I don't like	I like … / I don't like	I like … / I don't like	I like … / I don't like	I like … / I don't like

7.3   Families

LEVEL	**Beginners**
AGE GROUP	**8 and above**
TIME	**20 minutes**

DESCRIPTION

The children identify family members, add them to a family photo, and describe their relationship to the main character.

LANGUAGE

Vocabulary: family members: *dad, mum, brother, sister, grandma, grandad*. Grammar: possessive *'s*.

SKILLS

Writing: identifying and writing about family members.

ASSESSMENT CRITERIA

The children should be able to use the possessive *'s*, recognize 'family' vocabulary, and write sentences introducing family members.

MATERIALS

Worksheet 7.3 (see back of book); scissors; glue; overhead projector (optional).

PREPARATION

1 Photocopy Worksheet 7.3 for each child.

2 Enlarge a copy of the characters on Worksheet 7.3.

3 Set up the overhead projector if you are using one; if so, prepare a transparency of the completed worksheet for feedback.

IN CLASS

1 Show the children an enlarged copy of the characters at the bottom of the worksheet.

2 Explain that they are Mark and Judy and their family. The children have to guess who each person is, cut out the characters, and paste them into the right photo frame. Tell them to look for family resemblances such as freckles.

3 Hand out Worksheet 7.3 and ask the children to carry out the task.

4 Once they have finished, explain that they have to draw lines from each of the characters and write who they are, for example: *This is Mark's dad* or even simply *Mark's dad*.

5 The children complete the task.

FEEDBACK

1 The children compare answers with a partner to see if they agree. If there are any questions, they can ask them in an open class discussion.

2 Invite a couple of children who have arranged the family photos correctly to go round showing their work to their classmates for comparison. The children can then put the sentences they wrote, for example, *This is Mark's dad* or *Mark's dad* up on the board.

3   Alternatively if you have an overhead projector, put the final product on a transparency. You or the children can add the sentences as you go through the feedback.

FOLLOW-UP

1   The children can create their own imaginary family and talk about them. This could be a monster family or one based on familiar characters such as *The Simpsons*, *The Addams family*, etc.

2   They could also write sentences similar to the ones they used in the assessment task.

ASSESSMENT OF OUTCOME

1   After they have discussed their work with their partners, the children fill in a self-assessment form (see below).

2   While the children are filling in their forms, go round the classroom discussing their answers with them.

3   Finally, collect their worksheets and add your own comments: *Excellent, Very good*, etc. When you look at the completed task, have their self-assessment forms in front of you and add your comments on the assessment form as well, for example, *Yes, you did find the families. Well done! Be a little bit careful when you write. Don't forget the 's in* Mark's dad.

4   Give back the worksheets with the self-assessment form attached. The children can take them home for feedback from their parents.

Name _____ **Class** _____ **Date** _____

Families

I enjoyed doing this.	☺	😐	☹
I think I did well.	☺	😐	☹
I put the people in the right families.	☺	😐	☹
I explained who's who.	☺	😐	☹
I used the **'s** correctly.	☺	😐	☹

Circle the words you know.

dad   mum   grandad   grandma   sister   brother

PORTFOLIO   The completed worksheets, the self-assessment forms, and the follow-up work can be included in the children's portfolios if they wish.

7.4   We go together!

LEVEL	**Elementary**
AGE GROUP	**8 and above**
TIME	**10 minutes**
DESCRIPTION	The children match and copy sentences based on personal and possessive pronouns.
LANGUAGE	Personal and possessive pronouns.
SKILLS	Reading: recognizing relationships between sentences. Writing: copying sentences.
ASSESSMENT CRITERIA	The children should be able to recognize relationships between sentences with the help of personal pronouns: *This is Marta.* **She's** *from Mexico*, and relate personal and possessive pronouns to gender and number.
MATERIALS	Worksheet 7.4 (see back of book).
PREPARATION	Photocopy Worksheet 7.4 for each child.

IN CLASS

1 Hand out Worksheet 7.4.
2 Tell the children to look at part A of the worksheet and match the sentences that go together.
3 They then go to part B of the worksheet and copy the sentences under the right picture.
4 Collect the worksheets for checking.

FEEDBACK

1 Draw the pictures on the board. Ask the children to call out the sentences that go under each picture.
2 Before you write the sentences on the board, ask the children to explain why they chose each one.

FOLLOW-UP

Ask the children to make as many sentences as they can about the people in the pictures: *She's ten years old, She's got blue eyes*. These can be imaginary.

ASSESSMENT OF OUTCOME

Use a discrete-point marking-scheme. The children get two points for each correct sentence match and two points for each pair of sentences placed under the right picture.

8 Self-assessment

Children's self-assessment can include their attitudes towards learning and aspects of the learning process, such as the activities used by the teacher, the textbooks and other teaching materials they use, their preferred learning styles, and their actual progress/performance. The inclusion of all these areas in self-assessment signals their importance to the children. Most importantly though, self-assessment improves children's motivation, enjoyment, and understanding of important aspects of the language learning procedure, and offers them the basic skills that characterize autonomous learners, such as reflection on and regular review of their work.

The various types of self-assessment presented here are only intended as examples for you to try out and use as a springboard to create your own. You will probably have to go through an initial phase of experimentation until you find out what really works for your children. During this early phase you should also train the children in the basics of self-assessment since they may initially find it difficult. They need to be guided through the process and you will need to model how self-assessment works.

Moreover, in co-operation with the children, you need to set the criteria and illustrate what is considered acceptable, good, or excellent work, so that they understand what is expected of them. General self-assessment criteria can be set through discussion of what makes a good learner. When self-assessment focuses on achieving specific goals, you can discuss what *knowing* something means, for example, *I can say it, I can recognize it, I can understand it*, etc. You may be aiming for a specific level of 'knowing', such as recognition, and the children need to be aware of that.

It is also important that you arrange time to see their self-assessment entries and discuss them with each child. It may be possible to fill in easy-to-complete self-assessment worksheets, such as 8.1, in class. For others, you will need to find time soon after the children have completed their self-assessment. You can compare their assessment with your observations and their assessment task results to check whether their assessment is accurate. A private discussion with a child may not take more than a few minutes and could even take place just before or just after class. Finding time to make even a brief comment on the child's self-assessment is essential so that the children realize you are interested in what they think. Your feedback will also help to guide them in the right direction and help them to set goals that address difficulties identified during self-assessment.

If the children are having difficulties with language, you may have to use questionnaires in the mother tongue, although you could also try to use simple statements in language they have learned and practised, for example '*I like …*' rather than '*I enjoy…*', etc. Alternatively, you can use questionnaires to which the children respond with just a drawing. Go through questionnaires explaining the statements before getting the children to complete them. Depending on their level, you might ask the children to read the questionnaire statements in English, but allow them to write their comments and set their goals in their mother tongue. If the children are not yet able to read or write, read each statement, explain it, and then allow them time to complete their answer by choosing the right face on the page before moving on to the next statement.

Self-assessment documents should be kept in the portfolios so that the children can have access to their progress records whenever they wish. This way they are able to compare their progress at various points in their career. Encourage children to share self-assessment with their parents so that the parents can check their children's assessment and help them to set new goals. Self-assessment can be carried out at various strategic points during the course, and needs to be used as one among a variety of other assessment types.

8.1 Attitudes towards English lessons

LEVEL	**All**
AGE GROUP	**All**
TIME	**10 minutes** (when introduced for the first time; afterwards, two minutes at the end of each lesson)
AIMS	To encourage children to express their feelings and attitudes towards their English classes in a quick and efficient way.
DESCRIPTION	The children indicate their general feelings towards their English classes by drawing expressions on a face.
MATERIALS	Worksheet 8.1 (see back of book).
PREPARATION	Photocopy Worksheet 8.1 for each child. Modify it to suit your needs if you have lessons more or less frequently. Each face the children draw on the worksheet corresponds to one lesson. The day of the week should be written in the first column. In the last row, the children write something that made them happy (a song or a game, for example), thus strengthening their positive feelings towards the English classes.
IN CLASS	1 Draw a 'happy', 'sad', and an 'indifferent' face on the board and mime the feelings yourself.

2   Invite a few children to come to the board and draw other feelings they might have (angry, bored, etc.).

3   Tell the children that you would like them to think about the day's lesson and show you what they think about it by miming the expression that shows their feelings.

4   Hand out Worksheet 8.1 and explain it to the children.

5   Tell the children to look at the appropriate box and draw the face that best expresses their feelings about the day's lesson.

6   Collect the worksheets. Explain that they will be handed back to them at the end of every lesson for them to draw their feelings.

7   On the last lesson of the week, ask them to think of something that made them happy, so as to focus their attention on positive experiences.

8   Finally, at the end of the month, have them look at how many happy or sad faces they have on their worksheet. On the basis of the expression that seems to predominate for the month, they can decide what goes in the title, for example, *My English classes make me feel happy/sad/bored*, etc.

VARIATION

The worksheet can be adapted so that the children use it once a week or at other times, depending on your schedule and how often the children have English classes.

FEEDBACK

1   Ideally, try to review the worksheets and discuss each child's feelings at least once a fortnight in large classes and more often in small classes. Monitor the children's feelings so that you can prevent negative feelings and attitudes from becoming permanently entrenched.

2   Always make a point of finding out why the children are unhappy and take note of the things that make them happy, so that you can increase positive experiences and decrease negative ones.

PORTFOLIO

The completed weekly worksheets can be kept in the children's portfolios. They may be supplemented with interview notes, the children's notes, or observation notes on why a child was unhappy during a particular week, etc.

COMMENTS

1   It is very important to keep track of the children's attitudes towards their English classes. Prompt action when things don't seem to be going well may save both the child and you from a host of problems in the future.

2   Young children are sometimes influenced by things we might not consider important. We know of a motivated, happy child who suddenly didn't want to come to class any more. When asked what was making her unhappy, the problem turned out to be that a classmate had been pinching her! A promise that this would not happen again and an apology from the culprit resulted in her return to class.

3 Assign the responsibility for handing out the worksheets to one group of children a month. This way you can still carry on with the lesson while the group hands out the worksheets. The children return the worksheets to your desk on their way out.

8.2 Activity likes and dislikes

LEVEL

All

AGE GROUP

All

TIME

5 minutes

AIMS

To encourage children to express their feelings about various aspects of their English lesson and reflect on their preferred ways of learning.

DESCRIPTION

The children indicate how they feel about various aspects of their English lesson by filling in a questionnaire.

MATERIALS

Worksheet 8.2 (see back of book).

PREPARATION

Photocopy Worksheet 8.2 for each child. Modify it as necessary to suit your own teaching style and the learning procedures you frequently use in class.

IN CLASS

1 Tell the children you would like them to think about the various activities you do in class. Ask them to say which ones they like. Explain that this will help them to realize how they prefer to learn and it will also help you decide which activities you could do more often.

2 Hand out Worksheet 8.2 and make sure the children understand it.

3 Tell the children that they can circle whichever of the three faces best corresponds to their feelings about each specific aspect of learning English.

4 The children return their completed worksheets.

FEEDBACK

Look at the children's self-assessment in your own time, not too long after it was completed. You will sometimes need to make time to discuss the results individually, if a child doesn't seem to be enjoying anything.

PORTFOLIO

The self-assessment questionnaires can be included in the children's portfolios. You can also invite the children to elaborate, perhaps in their journals, listing the songs or games they like or explaining why they don't like a particular activity, for example, books.

8.3   A picture of achievement

LEVEL	**All**
AGE GROUP	**All**
TIME	**Throughout the course**
AIMS	To enable the children to develop criteria regarding their knowledge of English and to motivate them by providing a visual representation of their knowledge.
DESCRIPTION	The children gradually complete a picture by pasting in or drawing items according to the new language they have learned.
MATERIALS	Worksheets 8.3a, b, and c (see back of book); envelopes; coloured pencils; scissors; glue.

PREPARATION

There are three options for working with the picture.

1 Photocopy Worksheet 8.3a for each child if it suits your syllabus. The children colour in the things they have learned or draw other objects.

2 Use Worksheets 8.3b and 8.3c together. Worksheet 8.3c shows only the background outline. Worksheet 8.3b has pictures of the objects they are learning. You or the children cut out the objects on Worksheet 8.3b and keep them in envelopes labelled with each child's name, or you can store the worksheets in each child's portfolio. When the children need to use an item, they take it from their envelopes. You can also add other items.

3 The children can draw the items instead of using the ones provided. This gives flexibility for use with any syllabus. You could also choose another background thematically related to the course, for example, a park in London, a village, a beach, etc.

IN CLASS

1 At the beginning of the course, show the picture to the children and explain how it will be used. Tell them that they will be pasting in and colouring or drawing objects in the picture when they feel that they have learned something new.

2 Explain that at various points in the course, such as after an assessment task or the completion of a unit, they can decide if they are satisfied with their performance and if they have learned the language in question. For younger children this should be done with your help, whereas with older or more experienced children you may simply need to monitor their work.

3 Hand out the Worksheets. They can start by colouring the background and decorating the edge of the picture if they like.

4 The children store their Worksheets in their portfolios.

5 When the children have achieved an aim (for example, learnt the colours) you can open their envelope and give them the illustration that represents their achievement (for example, the rainbow) to stick on their picture; or give them Worksheet 8.3b so they can cut the rainbow out for themselves, or they can draw one.

6 For faster or more motivated children, you could provide additional elements for the picture, such as more food items, if they have learned a lot of new vocabulary. Children who have learned the names of ten to twelve animals can have three or four animals to paste onto the picture, whereas those who have learned only three or four may get only one. In this way each child completes their own unique picture and even the weaker children end up with a finished picture.

FEEDBACK

Look at and comment on their pictures whenever they add an item. Offer feedback on their progress.

VARIATION 1

Although the objects in this picture may be suitable for some courses, they will not be for others. The picture can be adapted by adding or removing items. You could use a completely different or more culturally relevant picture.

VARIATION 2

You might choose to use a thematically unrelated picture but one that appeals to the children. For example, for each achievement, you might add parts that will eventually make up a cute monster, a cartoon character, or the class mascot. The children can choose which part to add to the picture or the whole class can agree on parts at the beginning of a unit in a discussion. For example, *When we learn the colours what part shall we add to 'Cutie'?*

PORTFOLIO

1 This self-assessment can be a central element in their portfolio. The children keep the picture in their portfolios and decide on their own and/or after consultation with you what parts they are ready to stick on their picture. If the children are placing the items by themselves, check and discuss their progress regularly. This will help the children to develop their own criteria of what constitutes 'knowledge' of something.

2 The children might want to have a separate sheet attached to the picture, on which they add the evidence that they have learned a particular item, for example: *Colours: assessment task 4/11/2002.* Most of the time the evidence will be included in the portfolio anyway.

COMMENTS

1 This task helps the children to keep track of what they learn during the year. It is self-assessment carried out in a creative and non-threatening way. Each child has a picture to complete by adding different parts of the picture during the course.

2 Different parts of the picture can represent parts of the language syllabus, for example, structures (present continuous), functions (introducing yourself), or topics (colours, at the zoo). Where possible, the items in the picture should relate thematically to the structure, function, or topic they represent, so when the children know the names of animals this can be represented by a picture of one or more animals. Here are some examples of objects that can be thematically related to parts of the syllabus:

Structure/Topic/Function	Picture representing them
Family members	A family with a mother, father, brother, sister, sitting on the grass having a picnic
Food items	A picnic basket belonging to the family, with various food items: bread, fruit juice, fruit, cheese, etc.
Time	A sundial
Colours	The rainbow
The weather	Sun and/or clouds
Animals	One or more animals

8.4 Tortoise race

LEVEL	**All**
AGE GROUP	**All**
TIME	**15 minutes** (when introduced for the first time; afterwards, five minutes every unit or month)
AIMS	To enable children to develop a critical view of their learning progress and maintain or improve their progress rate over the year.
DESCRIPTION	The children assess their progress by placing their marker on a continuum. They compare and review their progress at different times during the year, so it becomes a race against themselves.
MATERIALS	Worksheet 8.4; scissors; 'blu-tack' or glue; (optional) animal stickers; overhead projector.
PREPARATION	1 Photocopy Worksheet 8.4 for each child. The worksheet can be used for self-assessment at the end of each unit or month.
IN CLASS	1 Remind the children of the story 'The tortoise and the hare' and emphasize the good qualities of the tortoise (patience, persistence).
	2 Hand out Worksheet 8.4.

3 Explain to the children that it will be used at the end of every unit or month (depending on what you choose) and how it will help them to review and track their progress regularly.

4 Demonstrate the use of the tortoise as an indicator of progress. On the board or overhead projector, put the tortoise on the extreme left of each lap if the children have not done too well, and on the far right if they have done very well.

5 Explain that at the end of every unit or month they will be asked to assess themselves by moving the tortoise to the point on the lap line representing their progress during that month or unit.

6 Discuss the assessment criteria and write them up on the board or overhead projector, for example:

Have I been attending class regularly?
Have I been listening to my teacher?
Have I been contributing to the lesson (asking/answering questions, participating in discussions)?
Have I been doing my homework?
Have I been reading English books?

7 Explain and discuss each point as you write it on the board.

8 Ask the children to think about the answers to the questions and to place their animal on the line according to how well they think they did over the period.

9 If they wish, they can discuss their decision with their partners or friends.

10 Tell the children to put the worksheet in their portfolios.

FEEDBACK

1 Look at their self-assessment in your own time, as soon as possible after the self-assessment was completed, but also allow time to discuss it with the children. Find out how the children reached their decisions and suggest ways of improvement.

2 Even if the children seem to be doing very well, make sure you comment on their entries so that they know their self-assessment is important to you.

VARIATION 1

You may decide to create an additional, final lap which the children complete to illustrate their progress throughout the year, and which sums up all their previous self-assessments.

VARIATION 2

You can also use other animals as markers.

PORTFOLIO	Worksheet 8.4 can be kept in the portfolios for the children to access whenever necessary. You may want to add notes from your discussions with the children or they might add a list of goals with dates (for example, to do their homework regularly), to help them to improve.
COMMENTS	1 The criteria finally agreed on during In class, step 6 can be written down and put on the notice board for reference in between self-assessments or at assessment times.
	2 If the discussion about criteria takes place in the mother tongue, you could simplify the criteria and write them in English. If you use them often the children will soon recognize their meaning. *Have I been attending class regularly?* can be simplified to *Do I come to class?* or *Do I come to my English lessons?*

8.5 Language skills

LEVEL	**All**
AGE GROUP	**10 and above** (see Variation for younger children)
TIME	**10 minutes**
AIMS	To encourage children to reflect on their competence in and attitudes to a specific language skill, to reflect on their learning strategies in that skill, to express feelings and thoughts on a specific language skill, and to set short-term goals for themselves.
DESCRIPTION	The children indicate their perceived competence in and their attitudes to a specific language skill by completing a questionnaire. They can also set short-term progress goals for themselves in that skill.
MATERIALS	A self-assessment questionnaire on the skill you are assessing (see the example on the next page).
PREPARATION	Prepare your own self-assessment questionnaire relevant to the skill you want to assess and to the level and syllabus of your class. The example on the next page focuses on reading. You may choose to have your questionnaire in the children's mother tongue.
IN CLASS	1 Hand out your questionnaire and explain the aims of this self-assessment task.
	2 Go through the statements with the children to make sure they understand them and know what to do.
	3 For part A, tell the children that they have to indicate to what extent they agree with the statements by drawing a mark on the line, as follows:

I can recognize English words I know	**a little**	___/___	**a lot**

4 For part B, the children write their comments and state their goals.

5 Allow the children to write their comments and their goals in their mother tongue or make yourself available to help them with words and expressions they don't know. For example: *I'll remember to read* Puss in Boots *next, Marko! I'm glad you like the stories we read in class.*

How good am I at reading?

Name _____ Class _____ Date _____

A

I can recognize English words I know when I see them.   **a little** _____ **a lot**

I can look at the pictures and understand
the story my teacher is reading to me.   **a little** _____ **a lot**

I can understand the stories read to me,
even when there are no pictures.   **a little** _____ **a lot**

I like having stories read to me.   **a little** _____ **a lot**

B

My comments   _____
_____

My goals for the next term: _____
_____

Teacher's comments

My signature _____   Teacher's signature _____

FEEDBACK

1 While the children are completing their questionnaire, go round and discuss it with the fast finishers. Ask them to support their decisions and help them to set realistic goals.

2 You can offer written feedback to the children by adding your comments to the worksheet.

PORTFOLIO

The worksheet can be kept in the portfolios. During portfolio reviews, discuss with the children whether they achieved the goals they set.

VARIATION

1 Questionnaires can be adapted to suit younger children or children who are only just beginning self-assessment. Use only part A of the questionnaire, not part B, which demands more independence and higher-level reflection.

2   The language of the statements in the first part can also be adapted according to the children's level.

COMMENTS

1   The four skills can be assessed separately not because they are discrete and unrelated, but because both the children and you may find it useful to reflect on them one skill at a time in order to focus on positive or problem areas.

2   This worksheet is only intended as an example of how self-assessment can address the language skills.

8.6 Coursebook-based self-assessment

LEVEL

All

AGE GROUP

All

TIME

10–15 minutes (after each unit in the coursebook)

AIMS

To encourage children to reflect on what they have learned in a specific unit; to recognize the focus of the unit.

DESCRIPTION

The children indicate the degree to which they have achieved the goals of a unit by completing a questionnaire.

MATERIALS

Worksheet in three parts: 8.6a, 8.6b, and 8.6c (see next page).

PREPARATION

1   Use the example on the next page to prepare a questionnaire that reflects your coursebook unit, and make copies of it.

2   The example uses pictures of vehicles associated with different speeds. You may choose animals or anything else to indicate the three different levels of achievement.

IN CLASS

1   Hand out the worksheet.

2   Tell the children that this questionnaire deals with how well they did in the unit they have just finished.

3   Go through the questionnaire step by step with the children and make sure they understand the statements. You may need to get the children to give examples of the language referred to in each statement, for example, *I haven't got a pencil*. Ask the children to remind you of the new words they learned, the games they played, etc.

4   Explain that for part A of the questionnaire they have to think about what they have been learning in this unit and decide how well they can do it, for example, say the colours. Tell them they can indicate their achievement by their choice of vehicle (aeroplane = very well, car = OK, bicycle = not so well).

5 Tell the children that in part B they have to write some new words they have learned. They are allowed to have their textbooks open during their self-assessment, so they can copy the words if they need to.

6 In part C, the children circle any of the faces that indicate their feelings towards some of the activities in the particular unit.

7 Give the children time to complete the questionnaires and reflect on their performance.

8 Assign a silent activity for fast finishers so that you have more time to observe and discuss with the children.

9 Go round the room and monitor the children's work. Answer possible questions and help the children if necessary.

Worksheet 8.6

Name _____	Unit _____	Date _____	
How well did I do in Unit 5?			
A	**Very well**	**OK**	**Not so well**
I can say what things I've got.	✈	🚗	🚲
I can say what things I haven't got.	✈	🚗	🚲
I can ask my friend 'Have you got a ...?'	✈	🚗	🚲
I know when to say 'Yes, I have.', 'No, I haven't.'	✈	🚗	🚲
I can count from 1–20 in English.	✈	🚗	🚲
I played the game on page 38.	✈	🚗	🚲

B I learned these new words: _____ , _____ ,

_____ , _____ .

C I liked the song. ☺ 😐 ☹

I liked the game. ☺ 😐 ☹

FEEDBACK	1 While the children are completing the questionnaire or working on their silent activity, go round and look at their questionnaires. Check how they completed them and if you agree with their perceptions. Comment on what they have achieved, either praising them or encouraging them to try harder.
	2 Older children can use their journals (see 8.7) and write a few goals based on their self-assessment. You can then comment and suggest ways to help them.
PORTFOLIO	The questionnaires can be kept in the children's portfolios. Evidence from assessment tasks focusing on the material taught in the specific unit can also be attached to this questionnaire.
COMMENTS	The self-assessment questionnaire presented here is based on Unit 5 of *Happy Street* by Stella Maidment and Lorena Roberts, OUP. Note that in part B of the questionnaire there is only room for four words even though there were six new words in this particular unit. This is so that children who have mastered fewer words will not feel they are underachieving.

8.7 Journal writing

LEVEL	**All**
AGE GROUP	**All**
TIME	**5–10 minutes** (at the end of a lesson every week or fortnight)
AIMS	To encourage the children to reflect on the language learning process in general. This assessment task emphasizes the children's feelings, thoughts, and personal experiences relating to their language learning.
DESCRIPTION	The children express their thoughts and feelings in a diary.
MATERIALS	An exercise book or folder with paper.
PREPARATION	The children can decorate their exercise books or folders.
IN CLASS	1 Explain to the children that they are going to start keeping a journal. Tell them they that can write or draw in it and that they can ask you for help when they need it. Depending on the children's language level, this is done in their mother tongue, at least initially.
	2 Negotiate your right of access to the children's journals. Explain that they will be private and that no one can read them without permission. This may be more of an issue with older children (10–12) in the first stages of puberty. Younger children are usually very eager to share with their teacher.

3   Show them some samples of journal entries to give them a better idea of what they are expected to do. Here is an example of a beginner-level child's journal entry, with the teacher's response:

Friday 15/3/2002

I like "The wheels on the bus".

I like "The wheels on the bus" too! It's one of my favourite songs.

4   Begin by asking the children to express in one sentence how they feel about the day's lesson (or their textbooks/homework/classmates).

5   Say that you will also keep a journal and model your journal entries the first few times the children use theirs. Write your journal entry publicly on the board and say your thoughts out loud as you do it. You can also model the use of drawings for the children to express their thoughts. With beginners, one or two sentences will be enough.

6   Allow the children time to write in their journals.

7   Ask who would like to share their journal with you. Take those journals home with you to read and respond to.

FEEDBACK

It is important to respond to the children's writing in a friendly way and to express genuine interest in what they have to say. This way the children will see that they have someone to share their thoughts and feelings with and that what they say really matters.

VARIATION

1   As the children become more experienced with journal writing and have more language at their disposal, you could suggest a number of questions which could, perhaps, be recorded permanently on the first sheet of the journal. These questions can help them to get started when they are having difficulties deciding what to write. Some guide questions are:

  – *What did you like best these last two weeks?*
  – *What didn't you like?*
  – *Do you enjoy your English lessons?*
  – *What do you like most?*
  – *What else would you like to do in your English lessons?*
  – *Did you use English this week? How? When? With whom?*
  – *What would you like to learn in the next few weeks?*
  – *Are you friends with your classmates?*

2   The questions will vary depending on the children's level and learning situation.

PORTFOLIO

1 Journal entries can sometimes be included in the children's portfolios. This should only be done if the child wants to include them, since the journal is primarily a private document.

2 Photocopy the journal entries that will go in the portfolios so you don't ruin the children's journals.

COMMENTS

1 Children need to be trained to use journals and your role is very influential in determining how successful they are. Although some teachers use journals as a way of assessing children's writing and its development over the academic year, the main aim of journal writing should always be to gain insight into children's attitudes to and perspectives on the learning situation.

2 It may take time for the children to accept the journal as part of their learning, but your response to their writing can speed things up. The children soon begin to enjoy this private method of communication between them and you. Through the children's responses to your additional clarifying/guiding questions, you can gain valuable insight into their individual learning preferences, attitudes, and abilities.

3 Journals can also help you establish a more private relationship with the children, one which is often impossible to create in large classes with tight timetables, where the children rush out of the classroom just as another group comes rushing in.

8.8 Speaking task performance

LEVEL

Elementary and above

AGE GROUP

8 and above

TIME

5 minutes (after the completion of selected speaking tasks)

AIMS

To encourage the children to assess their participation in interactive, pair, or group speaking tasks.

DESCRIPTION

The children indicate how they performed in a speaking task.

MATERIALS

Worksheet 8.8 (see next page); cassette (optional).

PREPARATION

Photocopy Worksheet 8.8 for each child. This worksheet can be very easily adapted to suit your speaking tasks.

IN CLASS

1 Before carrying out the selected speaking task, hand out Worksheet 8.8 to the children.

2 Tell the children that they are going to assess their own performance on the speaking task by using this questionnaire.

3 Go through the statements to make sure that they understand them.

4 Tell the children that they should circle the face that best expresses how they feel about each statement.

5 Allow the children to ask any questions they might have. (Steps 2–5 will not be necessary once the children get used to the procedure.)

6 The children carry out the speaking task.

7 The children fill in the questionnaire.

Worksheet 8.8

| Name _____ Unit _____ Date _____ | | | |
Name of task: _____			
I liked working with my friend/s.	😊	😐	🙁
I liked speaking in English.	😊	😐	🙁
I did the task.	😊	😐	🙁
I didn't make many mistakes.	😊	😐	🙁
I asked a lot of questions.	😊	😐	🙁
I answered my friend's questions.	😊	😐	🙁
I used only English.	😊	😐	🙁
I like the task.	😊	😐	🙁

FEEDBACK

1 You could invite the children to add more thoughts on how they performed and on the task itself when they write in their journals. This will give you the opportunity to find out more about how they did and to comment on their work.

2 If you recorded the speaking task, you can listen to the children and add your comments to their questionnaire on the basis of your assessment.

COMMENTS

1 This self-assessment task is particularly useful for speaking assessments where all the children come prepared and carry out the task, but you are only able to observe and assess two or four pairs or groups. The children who are not observed may feel their preparation and performance have not been appreciated. The children can fill in the questionnaire at the end of the task and later discuss it with you during a conference.

9 Learning how to learn

One of the main characteristics of successful learners everywhere is that they use learning-how-to-learn skills. When it comes to language learning, these skills include guessing meaning from context by using language, pictures, or the child's knowledge of the world, asking for help from others, and using a dictionary.

Sadly, these skills are not always promoted in the classroom and children are consequently disadvantaged by not being aware of the various language-learning skills and strategies available to them. Raising children's awareness of these strategies can greatly enhance their language learning potential. Learning-how-to-learn strategies can be developed from very early on and are especially important for young children, because they help them to form useful learning habits, and to become autonomous learners, thus benefiting every other area of their education.

Assessing learning-how-to-learn skills and strategies is one way of stressing the importance of these skills in the language-learning process. It may also encourage the practice and development of learning skills in other areas.

The assessment tasks presented in this chapter focus on just a few of the many learning strategies available. We have, however, tried to select strategies that can be useful and beneficial to the children.

The first assessment task in this section, 9.1, 'Using a dictionary to locate words', focuses on using a picture dictionary. If the children develop this skill further, you will eventually be able to extend the ideas and design assessment to include more advanced dictionary skills involving, for example, the use of English–English dictionaries.

Assessment tasks 9.2, 'Guess the word', and 9.5, 'My computer's gone crazy!', assess learning strategies that help enhance the children's receptive skills, so that they become better readers and listeners. Specifically, these tasks assess their ability to use linguistic and visual clues and other background information to understand the meaning of unknown words.

Assessment task 9.3, 'The princess and the dragon', assesses the children's ability to predict possible content. Making reasonably accurate predictions makes comprehension much easier, by helping the children to access their own relevant experience or knowledge of the world as well as their linguistic knowledge. This helps the children to prepare themselves for what they are going to hear and makes it easier to overcome the difficulties of facing unknown language.

Assessment task, 9.4, 'Taboo!', assesses paraphrasing. This important strategy allows children to deal with situations when they cannot find the words they need and have to compensate for gaps in their knowledge.

9.1 Using a dictionary to locate words

LEVEL	**Beginners**
AGE GROUP	**8 and above**
TIME	**10 minutes**
DESCRIPTION	The children find the English words for various objects.
LANGUAGE	Selected vocabulary.
SKILLS	Reading; using thematically organized picture dictionaries.
ASSESSMENT CRITERIA	The children should be able to find the English word for selected objects with the help of a picture dictionary.
MATERIALS	Worksheet; picture dictionaries.

PREPARATION

1 Make sure you have a sufficient number of picture dictionaries for the children to work with. The task can be carried out individually or in pairs. If there aren't enough dictionaries, you could assign the task to the children at different times in the lesson or over a number of lessons, so that everyone gets a chance to use a dictionary.

2 Select the words you want to use and prepare a worksheet for each child.

IN CLASS

1 Give out the worksheet you prepared to each child or draw pictures of the ten words you have selected on the board, for example:

How do you say this in English?

1 _____

2 _____

2 Make sure the children have access to the picture dictionaries.

3 Set a time limit of about seven minutes for the children to find the answers. Ask them to time themselves.

FEEDBACK

1 The children exchange worksheets, discuss their results and timing, help each other with any words they couldn't find, and correct each other's work.

2 Call out the best timings and award a small prize to the winners, for example, give them a round of applause or a sticker.

FOLLOW-UP

The children can prepare their own lists of pictures of objects. They then exchange lists with their partners and time each other on completing the task.

VARIATION 1

The activity may be done in a way that is less demanding and more suitable for younger children:

Write three things you can find:

In the park
_____

_____

_____

In the bathroom
_____

_____

_____

Photocopiable © Oxford University Press

VARIATION 2

The same activity can be carried out using a CD-ROM dictionary.

VARIATION 3

If you wish to use a learner-developed task, ask the children to prepare lists of picture objects by searching the dictionaries. Then mix up the lists and give them out randomly to the children. They find the objects in the dictionaries and find the English word for them.

ASSESSMENT OF OUTCOME

1 Use a discrete-point marking scheme. Award one point for each vocabulary item located.

2 Award a prize or bonus to children with fast timings.

9.2 Guess the word

LEVEL	**Elementary**
AGE GROUP	**8 and above**
TIME	**15 minutes**
DESCRIPTION	The children use pictures and context to guess the meaning of an unknown word.
LANGUAGE	Selected vocabulary.
SKILLS	Reading: guessing the meaning of a word with the help of visual aids and relevant context.
ASSESSMENT CRITERIA	The children should be able to use pictures and context to guess the meaning of unknown words.
MATERIALS	Worksheet 9.2 (see back of book).
PREPARATION	Photocopy Worksheet 9.2 for each child.

IN CLASS

1 Give out Worksheet 9.2.
2 Explain to the children that they have to read the sentences and guess the meaning of the words in **bold**. The pictures give four possibilities, but there is only one right answer.
3 The children have to tick or circle the right picture each time.
4 When they have finished the feedback, collect the worksheets.

FEEDBACK

Go through each sentence with the whole class. Ask the children to give you their answers with a show of hands. Ask them to explain why they chose the answers they did and why they excluded other possibilities.

ASSESSMENT OF OUTCOME

1 Use a discrete-point marking scheme. Award ten points, two for each correct answer.
2 Briefly discuss some answers individually with the children. Ask questions to help you understand how the child was thinking and also to help the children better understand how they can use pictures to help them, for example:

Why did you think _____ meant _____?
What would help you to find the right answer?

3 It is often difficult to find time to have private chats with all the children. Try to use the time when other children are looking at their results, or doing a silent activity, or the time you set apart for portfolio review. Nevertheless, if time is scarce, you may decide to chat with the children who seem to be having more problems than the others.

9.3   The princess and the dragon

LEVEL	**Elementary**
AGE GROUP	**8 and above**
TIME	**15 minutes**
DESCRIPTION	The children make predictions about the content of a story.
LANGUAGE	The usual language of fairy tales: *king, princess, dragon, fire, beautiful, palace, tower, land, prince.*
SKILLS	Listening: predicting content.
ASSESSMENT CRITERIA	The children should be able to make reasonable predictions based on the title and on the content of an oral text.
MATERIALS	Worksheet 9.3 (see back of book).
PREPARATION	Photocopy Worksheet 9.3 for each child and cut the copies along the dotted lines.
IN CLASS	

1 Tell the children that they are going to hear a story. Write the name of the story on the board.
2 Give out part A of Worksheet 9.3 to the children and ask them to think what kind of story they imagine this will be. They then circle five words they think will appear in the story.
3 Once the children have answered question 1, take in part A of the worksheet and start reading the story to them. When you get to the end of the first section (below) stop reading and ask the class to imagine what comes next.

Story script

> **The princess and the dragon**
>
> Once upon a time, in a country far away there was a beautiful princess. Her father, the king, was a very bad man. He didn't want his daughter, the princess, to be happy. So when the princess was fourteen years old, he locked her up in a secret tower in the palace and put a giant dragon in the tower to guard her.

4 Hand out part B of the worksheet. Read the options available for question 2 and make sure the children understand the meaning of the sentences.
5 Once the children have answered question 2, take in part B of the worksheet and continue with the following section of the story.

> The dragon didn't let anyone see the princess. No one ever visited her, and as the years went by she became more and more unhappy. She also became more and more beautiful, but she was so sad and so lonely that she cried all the time. Still the dragon never let her out.
>
> One day the dragon got sick and started crying. The princess heard him and asked him what was wrong.

6 Ask the children to imagine the rest of the story and hand out part C of the worksheet.

7 Ask question 3: *What do you think is going to happen next?* The children choose their answer.

8 Collect the completed worksheets and continue reading the story to the end.

> The dragon said that he was sick and that he couldn't fly or breathe fire because of the pain. The princess wanted to help him. She made him special drinks every day. Magic tea, and strong magic wine. After a few weeks the dragon got well again. He was very, very happy. He wanted to thank the princess for her kindness. So he took her with him and together they flew away to another country far, far away. The new country was full of kind, happy people. The princess stayed there and married a prince and lived happily ever after. And her friend the giant dragon stayed with them forever.

FEEDBACK

1 Feedback for question 1: Write the eight words on the board and ask the children to tell you which ones they guessed would be in the story and why. If no one mentions words like *school* or *zoo*, ask them why they didn't choose them. This will help them to understand the process of making reasonable predictions. Remember, however, that a child may suggest an unlikely word and may be able to justify it by producing his/her own development of events. In this case, accept the answer.

2 Feedback for questions 2 and 3: Ask the children to tell you what they thought would happen and compare the various stories that sprang from the children's imaginations. Accept all the stories and enjoy them!

3 Ask those who guessed the role of the dragon to tell you what made them predict this ending. With question 2 the direction of the story was not yet obvious. A reasonable prediction would have been that a prince would save the princess. After the next pause, however, there was reason to start thinking about the dragon as hero.

FOLLOW-UP

1 The children try to write their own fairy tales for homework. They then read them in class. They can stop after the title for the rest of the class to guess a few words they think will come up in the story. These words can be written on the board to be checked later. The child can also stop halfway through the story for the rest of the class to guess the ending.

2   If the children are not able to write their own story, give them the option to choose a story not known to their classmates and follow the same procedure.

ASSESSMENT OF OUTCOME

1   Question 1: The words linked to the story are: *king*, *prince*, *fire*, *beautiful*, *palace*. Award one point for each correct word.

2   Question 2: Give two points for a reasonable prediction. In this case, the story is a fairy tale and every option could be considered reasonable (anything is possible in fairy tales!).

3   Question 3: Give two points for a reasonable prediction. Although other options may be considered, the dragon is starting to have a leading role, thus indicating that he will play a big part in the princess's fate.

PORTFOLIO

1   Staple the three parts together and put them, along with their mark and your comments, in children's portfolios.

2   If the children keep a journal (see 8.7, 'Journal writing'), invite them to draw or write about the princess and the dragon. They can, for example, draw a scene from the story and add comments about it (in their mother tongue if necessary). They could also draw the ending they predicted and explain why they chose it and what really happened in the story. If the children do not keep a journal, their drawing can be done on a piece of paper and included in their portfolio.

9.4   Taboo!

LEVEL	**Pre-intermediate**
AGE GROUP	**10 and above**
TIME	**20 minutes**
DESCRIPTION	The children describe an object by paraphrasing.
LANGUAGE	Selected vocabulary.
SKILLS	Speaking: paraphrasing.
ASSESSMENT CRITERIA	The children should be able to use paraphrase in such a way that others can identify what is being described.
MATERIALS	Word cards.
PREPARATION	1 Prepare a set of 15 cards for each group of five children, with the names of objects and two words connected with each object (see

the example below). The aim of the activity is for the children to describe/define each object without using its name or either of the two descriptive words. These words are taboo! Choose words that will be easy for children to paraphrase!

2 The choice of taboo words can vary according to the children's level. Here is an example for elementary level:

Banana • fruit • yellow	Pencil-case • pencils • pens	Fork • eat • spoon
Sofa • long • furniture	Bicycle • ride • wheels	Toothbrush • teeth • clean
Sun • yellow • sky	Chicken • egg • bird	Aeroplane • fly • sky

Photocopiable © Oxford University Press

IN CLASS

1 Draw an example of a *Taboo!* card on the board and explain to the children that they have to define the word in **bold** (for example, **banana**) as best they can so that the members of their group can guess the word as fast as possible, but they are not allowed to use the word **banana** or the words under it. These words are taboo!

2 Divide the class into groups of five and give two cards to each player. Place five additional cards face down on the desk. Appoint a 'guard' from another group to make sure the children don't use any of the words on the cards. If they do, they lose.

3 Explain to the children that they have only a minute for each card and that they are collecting points for their team. When the minute is over, the turn goes to the next player. If the team finishes early, they can use the time to take turns using the cards on the table. Remind them of the time limit (which can vary according to the children's level).

4 The children should also take turns in acting as time-keepers for the rest of the group and as 'guards' for the other groups. For example, if a child was acting as a 'guard' for one round he or she returns to the group for the second round and is given two turns for missing the first round.

5 The children carry out the activity, taking turns to describe the object on their cards.

FEEDBACK

Give out a new set of cards and play the game with the whole class. Help the children to see similarities in the way they described objects and deduce some strategies for paraphrasing, for example:

We can talk about:
– shape and size

— what we can do with it
— where we find it/where it comes from

FOLLOW-UP

If you have time, ask children to prepare their own cards and play another round of *Taboo!* with the new cards.

VARIATION

Divide the children into pairs and give them the cards. Give the children a few minutes to prepare definitions. They are allowed to use a dictionary if they need to. They can then play the game in the same way.

ASSESSMENT OF OUTCOME

1 Award one point for each word the team guesses correctly. The 'guards' can be responsible for awarding points to the group they are guarding. They can later report to you.

2 Alternatively, use self-assessment: ask the children to draw a picture of themselves playing *Taboo!* They can also add captions or speech bubbles to express their feelings on their performance, for example:

3 The children can show their drawings to you and discuss or explain why they drew themselves the way they did. You can also use this opportunity to discuss their performance based on your observation notes.

PORTFOLIO

Although children may have added comments in their journals on other occasions regarding *Taboo!* (if they have played it in class before), encourage them to add their comments on how they feel about being assessed through *Taboo!* and on how well they think they have done. (See 8.7, 'Journal writing'.)

COMMENTS

Although the children should by now be familiar with the kind of tasks used for assessment, we would like to stress the importance of familiarity. If the children are playing *Taboo!* for the first time, they may find it confusing. Make sure they are comfortable with the activity before you use it as an assessment task. You may, for example, choose to have a 'warm-up' round of the game.

9.5 My computer's gone crazy!

LEVEL	**Pre-intermediate**
AGE GROUP	**10 and above**
TIME	**10 minutes**
DESCRIPTION	The children infer the meaning of a word based on the content of the sentence it is in.
LANGUAGE	Selected vocabulary.
SKILLS	Reading: guessing the meaning of a word, relying solely on text.
ASSESSMENT CRITERIA	The children should be able to infer the meaning of a word based on the content of a sentence.
MATERIALS	Worksheet 9.5 (see next page); overhead projector (optional).
PREPARATION	Photocopy Worksheet 9.5 for each child.

IN CLASS

1 Explain that your computer has a problem and that every now and then it changes a word you type. In Worksheet 9.5 you forgot what the word typed was. The children have to read each sentence and guess the meaning of the strange word. Although it is preferable for them to write the word in English, they are allowed to write it in their mother tongue if they do not remember the English one. There may be more than one possible answer. If their answer makes sense, accept it.

2 Give out Worksheet 9.5 to each child.

3 The children carry out the task.

4 Collect the worksheets for checking.

FEEDBACK

1 Either give the children another copy of the worksheet for them to go through and fill in the correct answers with you, or write the sentences on the board, or use a transparency of the worksheet on an overhead projector. In each case, the whole class discusses the answers.

2 Go through each sentence together. It is helpful if you ask them to explain why they chose that particular word and why they excluded other possible words. This helps the children who made a mistake to understand why their choice is wrong. It also helps children to practise sound reasoning.

Worksheet 9.5 My computer's gone crazy

Name _____ Class _____ Date _____

My computer's gone crazy! Can you help to correct the word I typed?

1   My name's Sophie. I live in London. I have one brother and one ljsflfjsl. _____

2   Jane looks very pretty today. She is wearing a beautiful jflsjlfsjlfsl. _____

3   Let's go and eat. I'm very hlajfhwourosi. _____

4   Carlos lives in a house with a big dldjpirep. _____

5   I feel very tired. I'd like to go to jfossqu. _____

6   It's cloudy today. We'll need an ajfhsdjhf. _____

7   Have you got a camera? Let's take a kjutwsdjhfe. _____

8   I don't feel well. I've got a kjgskjerw. _____

9   Ahmet went to the diuikjks to buy some fruit. _____

10   Giovanni's grandmother has a beautiful garden with lots of jgafhdfhsa. _____

Photocopiable © Oxford University Press

FOLLOW-UP

1   The children can try to create similar exercises, with perhaps one or more sentences each. This can also be done as homework.

2   Divide the class into two groups. The children take turns to read their sentences. They pretend to be broken tape recorders and go bzzzz when the strange word comes along. Members of the opposite group try to find the answer. The groups get a point for each correct answer.

3   If there is no time to play this game in class, pass a sheet of lined paper round the class and ask the children to write down one or two of the sentences they prepared. Photocopy this paper for the children to identify the strange words either for homework or as additional class work for fast finishers.

ASSESSMENT CRITERIA

Use a discrete-point marking scheme out of 20. Give two points for each plausible answer. Do not deduct points for spelling mistakes.

Possible answers:
1   sister
2   dress/jacket/hat
3   hungry
4   garden
5   sleep/bed
6   umbrella
7   photo/picture
8   headache/toothache/stomach ache
9   supermarket/greengrocer's
10   flowers

10　Record keeping and reporting

Introduction

In this section we provide some ideas on how to keep a record of and report children's progress. The richest and most informative records of a child's progress are kept in the child's portfolio, which should form the basis of your reports on the child's progress. The reports should also be included in the portfolio, and become part of the child's overall assessment during portfolio review. When children keep their reports in their portfolios, they can study your feedback whenever they wish to, thus taking stock and keeping their efforts focused in the right direction. Finally, it allows them to compare their results at different points in the year and evaluate their progress.

Reports to children can usually be addressed to the parents as well, but there may be cases where children and parents could receive different reports, for example, with very young children who cannot read extensive comments even in their mother tongue. You can give them reports with very little or no language but pictures instead. Reports addressed to parents should avoid technical terms and should both inform parents on the children's progress and invite their participation in the learning and assessment process. Reports addressed to children and/or parents can provide space for feedback from them. Both children and parents can use this opportunity to indicate that they understand the assessment outcome as well as to make suggestions to the teacher or perhaps add their own opinions of the report results.

This chapter offers a variety of examples of record keeping and reporting. We do not expect that you will adopt all the reports as they are. Rather, you can easily adapt them to suit your particular needs and settings, and create your own reports if necessary. How often you give reports depends on your teaching situation, but it usually takes place two to four times a year. You will decide which reports to use depending on the goals of your course, the number of children, the duration of the course, your educational system and philosophy, and, of course, your own personal preferences.

10.1   Term/semester report

Rationale

This report provides space for you to comment on skills and attitudes as well as on other possible categories such as homework. If your coursebook emphasizes specific skills or other categories you can adjust the report. Reporting on attitudes means making use of observation as well as other assessment methods.

Space is also provided for the children's and parents' comments, since this is a way to encourage their active involvement in the assessment process and gets them thinking seriously about the learning process. As a result, the children can develop an understanding of their weaknesses and may use the comments section to commit themselves to a course of action or simply express their feelings about their assessment. Parents, on the other hand, may use their comments to show their appreciation of the teacher, comment on their own perception of their child's progress, or state their willingness to be more involved.

How to use it

1   Photocopy Worksheet 10.1 at the back of the book. You can use this report at the end of each term/semester and/or at the end of the year. In the 'skills' section you may want to write comments on the children's progress in a particular skill and include evidence from your observations as well as other assessments of this skill, make references to work samples in the children's portfolios and, if relevant, suggest a course of action. In the attitude section you can comment on the children's attitudes to English, their behaviour in class, and their co-operativeness or lack of it.

2   The report provides a space for a mark or grade and also for additional comments that may not correspond to any of the other categories (you might, for example, want to comment on the children's progress since their last report).

3   Give the report to the children, preferably when the parents are also present, so that you can discuss it with them and clarify anything that is not clear. In this way you avoid misunderstanding, or misinterpretation, of your comments on the part of the children or parents.

4   The discussion can also help and prepare the children and parents to complete their comments on the report. Younger children may not be able to comment on their assessment or if they do, their comments may not be substantial. In this case, omit the section for children's comments. If, however, children and parents do comment on the report, respond to them promptly while the report is still fresh in their minds. The report can then be kept by the children in their portfolios.

10.2 Term report with emphasis on attitudes

This report provides space for rating the four skills as well as six categories on attitudes and motivation. You may find it more useful for the first years of language learning because the emphasis on these non-linguistic categories demonstrates to the children how important they are in language learning. Understanding their importance at an early stage can potentially speed up the learning process in the long run.

At the same time the inclusion of general descriptors (very good, good) may be less threatening and consequently more motivating to young learners than a letter or number grade.

How to use it

1 Photocopy Worksheet 10.2 at the back of the book. On the basis of your records, tick the most suitable description. Add comments on any aspects you consider necessary. More general comments can be included in the overall comments section.

2 Again, this form of report highlights the importance of involving the children and the parents and provides space for their own comments. These comments can be added after a discussion with you.

10.3 Class progress chart

Rationale

It is often useful to have a progress chart for the whole class. One look and you can spot who is falling behind, who is keeping up, and who seems to be racing ahead. This enables you to prepare additional work for the children who seem to need more, as well as extra work for those who need to be stretched. An overall progress chart is also a good way of evaluating your own work. If, for example, the majority of the children do not seem to have achieved the aims you set for the term, you perhaps need to look at factors other than the children themselves. It may be that the materials you use, your teaching pace, your methodology, and/or the way you implemented it have influenced the outcome.

The sample class progress chart given here is designed to be used throughout the year and covers progress on attitudes, the four skills, and learning skills and strategies. (See photocopiable Worksheet 10.3 at the back of the book.) In this chart, progress in the four skills is based on the profile of a child in his/her second year of learning English. The points in the attitudes and learning skills categories can be used for children of any age or level. You may need to change or adapt the various categories to suit your particular needs.

How to use it

1 Photocopy Worksheet 10.3 at the back of the book. The chart has room for you to record progress for up to 15 children. If you have a larger class, you can make more copies or add more columns (each column corresponds to one learner).

2 Since the chart reflects the children's progress throughout an academic year, you could complete it at the end of each term, indicating the children's progress with practical symbols such as ★ (excellent progress), ✓ (very good progress), or ✗ (unsatisfactory progress) or other symbols which may be more meaningful and practical for you. Progress symbols for each term/semester could be registered in different colours, for example, red for autumn term/semester, etc.

3 Although it is possible to assess the achievement of many of the aims with the help of the portfolio and other assessment tasks, there are aims for which your decision will be based on your observations of the children.

4 The class progress chart can be kept in your file for your own reference but can also be used when you need to report progress to other colleagues or the school management. It can also be handed to the teacher who will be taking over your class next year. There may be times when you need to show the chart to parents, for instance, when you are discussing a learner's lack of progress and need to produce some comparative evidence. In this case, be careful not to show the parent the other children's names. What is important is not individual names but evidence of overall class progress.

10.4 Report focusing on an individual skill: speaking

Rationale

Sometimes we want to report on a single skill so as to focus and report progress on that particular skill, analysing the children's development in detail. It also helps to draw the parents' and the children's attention to that skill, making them understand its importance and the work involved in its development.

Although you may think it is a lot of work to fill in four different reports, one for each skill, it is not necessary to do it very often. You might only do them twice a year, once at the end of the first term/semester to focus the parents' and children's attention on the individual skills, and once at the end of the year to report progress. However, if children are particularly weak in a given skill, it may be a good idea to complete reports on that skill more regularly to encourage progress. Here we include an example of a report focusing on speaking. Other skills can also be assessed with similar reports.

How to use it

Photocopy Worksheet 10.4 (below). This report is open-ended. The sections include:

Attitudes towards communicating orally in English. Attitudes are perhaps more important in oral communication than in any other area. Negative attitudes towards the teacher, the class, English itself, or even fear of using the language if they don't feel competent, may result in children refusing to speak. Children have to feel comfortable expressing themselves orally from very early on. Assessment points to include in the report are the children's willingness to participate in the classroom, to volunteer answers, to initiate conversation, and their enjoyment of rhymes or songs.

Speaking skills development level. This section can be completed on the basis of the aims you set for a specific term. You can comment on what the children have achieved and what they still need to work on, for example, *Svetlana can recite rhymes and she can say short sentences in English.* You may sometimes need to simplify the aims so that they are comprehensible and relevant to the parents.

Strategies used. The strategies used in speaking are an important part of speaking ability. They are essential, even for native speakers. Children may start by using strategies such as asking for help, coining a word, or using gestures. They may also resort to their mother tongue in the early stages. This is acceptable provided we also encourage them to use strategies based on the target language.

Goals to be achieved. Set manageable goals for the children to aim for and include ideas on how parents can get involved. If children are shy, you might suggest getting them started with songs and rhymes, which they almost always enjoy and which may give them greater confidence in speaking. Other ideas are for the parents to help their children to record themselves when practising, or to act out little sketches with them.

Worksheet 10.4

Name _____ Term/semester _____ Class _____ Date _____

1 Attitude to communicating orally in English

2 Speaking skills development level

3 Strategies used

4 Goals to be achieved

Teacher's signature _____

10.5 Child-oriented report A: Happy flowers

Rationale

The Happy Flowers report is an example of a child-oriented report. (See Worksheet 10.5 at the back of the book.) Although this particular design may appeal more to very young children or older girls, the same kind of report can be designed differently, with three or more trees, beach umbrellas, houses, clowns holding balloons, etc.

Child-oriented reports acknowledge children's right to be informed on their progress and to be treated as equal partners in the learning process. These reports also encourage children to view their progress critically and to recognize what they are expected to be able to do versus what they can do. The visual aspect of the report also helps children to quantify and visualize their knowledge. Worksheet 10.5 (see back of book) can be used for all four skills by inserting the name of the skill in the blank, for example, *I can speak/listen to/read/write English*. The example given here focuses on speaking.

The aims are simplified so that they are meaningful to the child and so that even weaker children can complete it and be proud of their achievements. Some children may be able to talk about six things, for example, but even with four a child can complete a flower. Below that level, however, the children will recognize their weaknesses and realize they have to try harder. They can always go back and complete their flower the following term.

The report can show the children's development over a term/semester or an academic year. If you use it for a whole academic year, each flower includes the aims for a term/semester (three flowers correspond to three terms). The same report design can, of course, be adapted to different courses and syllabi. It can also be used in topic-based courses: each flower then represents things a learner can do around a particular topic. The report can be given to the child at the end of three topic units. The aims achieved can be inserted on the leaves or the centre of the flowers. The petals can be used for the children to add examples (see the illustration). Use the leaves to show aims that the children won't have concrete examples for.

How to use it

1 The report can be used at the end of each term/semester. It remains in the children's portfolios so that they can easily access it for review. The report can be completed in the following ways:

Teacher-completed report
When you are completing the report, add the aims the child has achieved (these aims may spread over two or more flowers/terms). Discuss it with the child who, in turn, colours in the aims achieved.

However, you can only complete the main aspect of the aim achieved, for example, '*I can ask and answer questions*'. Find time to conference with the child, discuss the report, and ask him/her to help you to complete the petals by giving you specific examples of what he/she can do (see the conference extract below, where a child and teacher are talking about the aim 'I can say …').You are thus enabling the children to contribute so that the report becomes personalized and expresses what the children think they can do.

Conference extract

Teacher	So I wrote this here because I think you can say a lot of things. What can you say? Can you tell me a few things in English?
Child	Ball, cat …
Teacher	Yes … Shall we write these down? In the flower petals?
Child	Yes.
Teacher	OK, I'll write what you say on this paper and then you can copy it. OK?
Child	OK.
Teacher	Ball, cat …what else?

Child-completed report

The children can complete the report in two ways.You can give them either the report with the aims already completed or a blank report.

2   When the children are involved in preparing their reports, it is best not to let all of them do it at the same time, or class chaos ensues. Divide the class into groups. Each group completes the report while the rest of the class is busy with silent activities.This gives you time for individual conferencing.

3   If you use the report with the aims filled in, ask the children to read the report and decide which things they can do.When they are ready, chat with them and check their perceptions, helping them to be realistic. Once the aims are decided the children can colour them in.Then encourage the children to give you examples of what they can do in relation to these aims, for example what they can say, what songs they can sing (see conference extract above).Write down the examples they give you so that they can copy and complete their reports.

4   If you use a blank report, write the main aims on the board, divided into the three sections/terms corresponding to the flowers. Ask the children to think about what they can do. After discussing it with you, they copy the main aims on to their reports. Continue as in Step 3.

10. 6   Child-oriented report B: Athletes on the podium

Rationale

This is another example of a child-oriented report (see 10.6 at the back of the book). The only difference is that this format includes only the aim, not examples. This time the design may appeal more to boys, but again it can be modified to suit your children's interests. The benefit of this design is that every child becomes a medal winner. Even if children do not manage to cover all the aims by the end of the year, they may still feel that something has been achieved because they are bound to have reached a medal stage, whether it is gold, silver, or bronze. Present the children with prizes, such as paper medals on a string, to reward their achievement. By the end of the year, children may have achieved different levels in each term. They get the medal from the highest one, unless you decide that they worked less hard one term, for example.

How to use it

1   Photocopy Worksheet 10.6. If the report is kept in this or a similar format, it can be completed at the end of each term/semester and the children can keep it in their portfolios. The aims you write on each podium represent the aims of each term/semester (i.e. 3 podiums = 3 terms).

2   Complete this report in the same way as 'Child oriented report A: Happy flowers report' (see Worksheet 10.5). Either you complete it and give it to the children or they complete it themselves.

3   If the children are completing it themselves, write up the aims for each term on the board so they can choose which ones they have achieved. After they conference with you they write them down.

4   Alternatively you could give the children a completed report on which they mark the aims they achieved.

10.7   Course-specific progress report

Rationale

Most of the examples of reports and record keeping in this book are based on children's anticipated language development, the basic stages they go through, and the basic skills that need to be developed. Nevertheless, we often use course-specific reports, and Worksheet 10.7 (see back of book) is an example, based on the assessment of Units 1 and 2 of *Happy Street* 1 by Julia Maidment and Lorena Roberts. Course-specific reports can be used at the end of a certain number of textbook units, at the end of a term/semester, or at the end of the year.

Such reports include the objectives of the course, which can be reported in terms of what the child can do, for example, *Soren can ask the way*. This makes the report relevant and meaningful to the children and their parents. The children can also see a direct relationship between their work in class and their progress report. Assessment results should be motivating by being expressed in positive statements indicating how well a child can perform.

This sample report focuses on progress in all four skills because the units themselves deal with all four skills simultaneously. But you could choose to spend less time on a particular skill or not assess it at all, in which case omit the particular skill from the report. If, for example, the child's mother tongue uses a script radically different from the Latin (for example, Arabic, Chinese, Korean, Thai, etc.), you may prefer to delay assessing writing.

Course-specific reports should also include comments on children's attitudes and effort. These aims are essential in education. There is no better way for children to recognize their importance than to see them featuring first on their progress report.

How to use it

1 In order to prepare a course-specific report, use the instructional goals which appear in the coursebook syllabus.
2 Circle one of the three faces in each category to indicate the children's progress. Base your judgement on the results of assessment tasks you have used, observations you have made, and the children's portfolio entries.
3 Before distributing the report, explain what each face represents. For example, you can say ☺ means that you are very pleased with the children's performance and that the children have achieved the particular aim very well. ☺ means that the children are doing OK, though there is still room for improvement, and ☹ means that the children are having problems in this area and should try harder.
4 The children study the report, discuss it with you, and add comments if they wish to.

10.8 Class observation

Rationale

During any lesson we observe children all the time and obtain important information on all aspects of their performance, attitudes, and motivation. When it comes to attitudes and motivation, observation yields much better results than any questionnaire. To create a learner profile, information from observation should complement other assessment tasks. Observation can also help you to identify children who react negatively and fail in paper-and-pencil assessments, although they regularly succeed in performing the same tasks in class.

We cannot be completely fair to children and parents unless we systematically record our observations. It is easy to remember times when children were particularly disruptive or angelic, but it is all too easy to forget the behaviour of average children or the times when usually unprepared children made special efforts in their work or class contribution. In large classes it is also possible to overlook the quiet children at the back of the class.

We can usually solve these problems if we use a written observation record rather than trying to keep mental notes. Worksheet 10.8 is an observation record sheet with categories for attitudes, learning, and communication skills, as well as the four language skills. The first three can be used with any level, whereas the four skills categories in this example are more closely linked to the developmental stage of a Year 2 learner and limited to categories that can be easily and adequately assessed through observation.

How to use it

1 If observation notes are going to be part of your assessment, it is a good idea to tell the children so at the beginning of the year. It is important for them to know what counts in their assessment. They also need to know that what makes a good learner is not just the results of assessment tasks but their performance in class as well.

2 The record sheet is designed to be used with five children at a time. (See photocopiable Worksheet 10.8.) It is difficult to focus your attention on a large number of children and make valid observation notes. It is better to concentrate on a small number of children each lesson who are sitting in the same area of the classroom. This makes observing easier and is more practical if you want to observe them during group work.

3 Be ready to record any interesting information about children who did something worth noticing on another day. For this, it is useful to keep the observation sheets in your file.

4 The record sheet has a large number of categories. It is unlikely that you can report on all the categories after only one lesson. You may find you need to come back to a group of children a number of times, so put the date at the top of the column for each observation entry you make.

5 Add your observation notes using practical symbols such as:
   • = adequate achievement of this aim
   + = moderate achievement of this aim
   – = inadequate achievement of this aim
   ? = there were no opportunities to observe performance in this aim.

6 You may sometimes be able to jot down a note while still in class, but most of the time this will not be possible. Do, however, allow yourself time to complete your observation record as soon as possible after the class and preferably before you start the next class.

7 You could collaborate with a colleague to cover each others' classes while you are making observations.

8 You could also video your class if you have the equipment.

10.9 Speaking task report

Rationale

This example is used to report on children's performance in an interactive speaking task for pairs or groups. It is presented here in two variations. 10.9a is suitable for beginners and elementary level children, and 10.9b is more suited to pre-intermediate children and above. (See photocopiable Worksheets 10.9a and b at back of book.)

The lower-level speaking task report (10.9a) concentrates on three categories: fluency, task achievement, and pronunciation.

The higher-level speaking task report (10.9b) has two additional categories: appropriateness and discourse management.

– Both reports divide each category into three performance levels and describe the child's performance in each category so that it is easy for you to decide the child's performance level.

– You can use blank columns if you want to avoid a child seeing his/her performance in relation to other levels or if you want to include other aims or details in the categories.

Both reports allow you to add your comments either for a particular category or generally on the child's speaking skills or attitudes to speaking. They also allow you to suggest a course of action for improvement.

How to use it

1 It is impossible to assess the speaking performance of a whole class at the same time. Try to focus on and assess a few groups or pairs of children at a time.

2 You can either use recordings of the children's performance or assess them while observing them carrying out the task.

3 Once you are familiar with the report and the different levels of performance it is very easy to use while, or just after, observing the children. The practical benefit of this report is that it incorporates a marking scheme. By ticking the level the child has attained and adding a few comments, the report is ready.

10.10   Writing task report

Rationale

Although younger learners may not yet be able to write beyond sentence level, 10–12-year-olds are often able to write paragraphs or simple stories. If the writing task includes an element of freedom, a marking scheme and report are useful.

This report deals with four aspects: accuracy, task achievement, handwriting, and mechanics. At different stages we may need to emphasize different aspects of writing and you can adapt the report to suit your needs.

This report is useful when you are assessing writing at paragraph level and above, and are not simply using writing as a means to assess grammar and/or vocabulary.

How to use it

1   Photocopy Worksheet 10.10 at the back of the book. You can adapt it to suit your needs, then tick the child's performance in each area. You can add further comments relating to specific areas in the right-hand column, and overall comments at the bottom.

2   You can complete the 'Action suggested' section after a discussion with the child, in which case the child can also sign the report.

Name _____ **Class** _____ **Date** _____

Name _____   **Class** _____   **Date** _____

Name _____ **Class** _____ **Date** _____

Name _____ **Class** _____ **Date** _____

A

Listen and tick (3) the words you hear.

eggs ❏   juice ❏   plate ❏   bananas ❏   biscuits ❏

water ❏   bowl ❏   yoghurt ❏   apples ❏   fruit ❏

strawberries ❏   glasses ❏   oranges ❏   kiwi ❏

B

Listen and put the words in the order you hear them.

mash _____

stir _____

decorate _____

cut _____

pour _____

WORKSHEET 2.5 CRAZY WEATHER

Name _____ **Class** _____ **Date** _____

How was the weather on Mary's holidays? Listen and write the day under each picture.

| Monday, | Tuesday, | Wednesday, | Thursday, | Friday, | Saturday, | Sunday |

Wednesday

A Name _____ **Class** _____ **Date** _____

Colour your monster's head, hands, teeth, and eyes.
Use only green, blue, and red.

✂ -

B Name _____ **Class** _____ **Date** _____

Colour your monster's head, hands, teeth, and eyes.
Use only orange, yellow, and brown.

Name

Class

Date

WORKSHEET 3.5c WHO'S GOT MY SHOPPING?

chocolate cake
chicken
soap
bananas
ketchup

MILK

SOAP

WORKSHEET 3.5d WHO'S GOT MY SHOPPING?

- biscuits
- shampoo
- cat food
- lamp
- jam

WATER

CHOCOLATE CAKE

SHAMPOO

WORKSHEET 3.5a WHO'S GOT MY SHOPPING?

- a pencil
- chocolates
- milk
- sweets
- apples

CHOCOLATES

LEMONADE

KETCHUP

WORKSHEET 3.5b WHO'S GOT MY SHOPPING?

- Orange juice
- Lemonade
- a sandwich
- crisps
- water

Orange juice

Crisps

JAM

BISCUITS

Surname _____	**Surname** _____ Figo _____
Name _____ Luis _____	**Name** _____
Year of birth _____ 1972 _____	**Year of birth** _____
Country _____	**Country** _____ Portugal _____
Height _____	**Height** _____ 1.81m _____

Surname _____	**Surname** _____ Zidane _____
Name _____ Zinadine _____	**Name** _____
Year of birth _____ 1972 _____	**Year of birth** _____
Country _____	**Country** _____ France _____
Height _____ 1.85m _____	**Height** _____

Surname _____ Beckham _____	**Surname** _____
Name _____	**Name** _____ David _____
Year of birth _____ 1975 _____	**Year of birth** _____
Country _____	**Country** _____ England _____
Height _____ 1.80m _____	**Height** _____

Surname _____	**Surname** _____ – _____
Name _____	**Name** _____ Ronaldo _____
Year of birth _____	**Year of birth** _____ 1977 _____
Country _____ Brazil _____	**Country** _____
Height _____ 1.81m _____	**Height** _____

Surname _____	**Surname** _____ Carlos _____
Name _____ Roberto _____	**Name** _____
Year of birth _____ 1974 _____	**Year of birth** _____
Country _____	**Country** _____ Brazil _____
Height _____	**Height** _____ 1.68m _____

Name _____ **Class** _____ **Date** _____

| lions | gorilla | elephants | penguins | foxes |
| giraffes | crocodiles | snakes | hippos | ponies |

Name _____ **Class** _____ **Date** _____

pony	snake	lion	elephant	fox

giraffe	gorilla	crocodile	penguin	hippo

I know these animals:

_____

_____

_____

_____

_____

_____

_____

_____

I will try harder to learn these animals:

_____

_____

_____

_____

_____

_____

_____

_____

Name _____ Class _____ Date _____

The sky is pink.

The clouds are yellow.

The grass is orange.

The trees are purple and the fruit is blue.

The flowers are black.

The river is white.

The cows are red.

Name _____ **Class** _____ **Date** _____

Read and draw

This is my grandma's garden. There's a pond in the middle of the garden. There are three ducks in the pond. Behind the pond there's an apple tree. There are five big apples under the tree! Today, there are two big birds in the tree. Look at my grandma's house. It's got two small windows. Ginger, her cat, is on the roof and Spot, her dog, is sitting in front of the door.

Edinburgh Zoo

WHAT CAN YOU SEE?

◆ over 1,000 animals – with fur, feathers, and scales – from all over the world

◆ see the penguins underwater in the world's biggest penguin pool

◆ watch the penguin parade every day at 2.00 p.m.

◆ meet the new animals: a family of meerkats

WHAT CAN YOU DO?

◆ get really close to small animals such as snails, rats, and snakes

◆ meet the keepers and learn about interesting and endangered animals

◆ find out more about animals: touch their bones, horns, teeth and skins

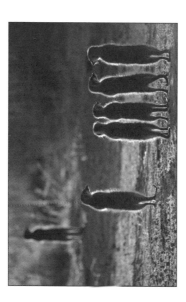

Special events

Easter Treasure Trail
30 and 31 March
Follow the animals' clues and find a chocolate surprise!

Rhino Week
17–26 May
Games and fun to help raise money for wild rhinos

'Into Africa' summer school
21 July – 15 August
For children aged 6–14. Go on a safari round Africa in the zoo!

Art at the Zoo
27 July – 5 September
Colourful and exciting paintings of animals

Enquiries
For details of all events and our education programme, please telephone:
0131 334 9171

Name: _____

Class: _____

Date: _____

1 Give the name of one special event at the zoo.
_____

2 How many animals are there at the zoo?
_____

3 What's happening between 17th and 26th May?
_____

4 What is the telephone number for enquiries?
_____

5 What time can you watch the penguin parade?
_____

Name _____ **Class** _____ **Date** _____

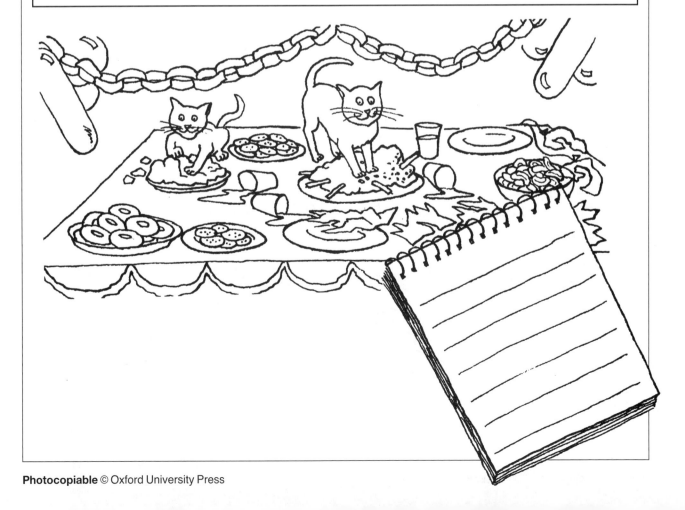

party hats, chocolates, balloons, burgers, crisps,
candles, jelly, birthday cake, drinks,
doughnuts, biscuits, sandwiches

Name _____   **Class** _____   **Date** _____

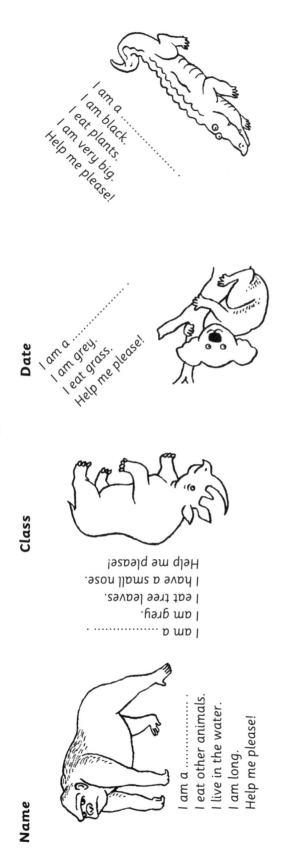

Help us!!!

Class **Date**

I am a ....
I am black.
I eat plants.
I am very big.
Help me please!

I am a ....
I am grey.
I eat grass.
Help me please!

I am a ....
I eat tree leaves.
I have a small nose.
Help me please!

I am a ....
I eat other animals.
I live in the water.
I am long.
Help me please!

A Name

Help us!!!

Class **Date**

I am a ....
I am white.
I eat fish.
I am very big.
Help me please!

I am a ....
I am black and white.
I eat bamboo.
Help me please!

I am a ....
I eat small fish.
I live in the sea.
I am blue.
Help me please!

I am a ....
I am yellow and black.
I eat other animals.
I am a big cat.
Help me please!

B Name

162   WORKSHEET 6.1c

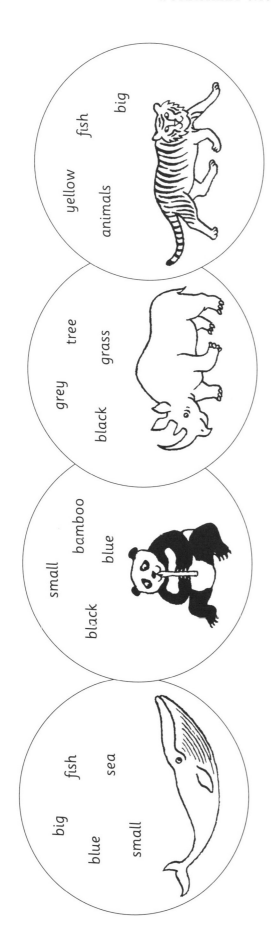

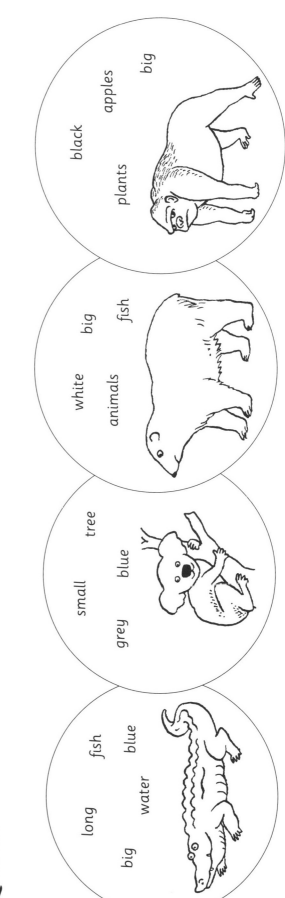

Colour the cats under the car black
Colour the cats in the car brown
Colour the cats on the car yellow

Colour the birds in the sky blue
Colour the birds on the house red
Colour the birds under the tree orange

A

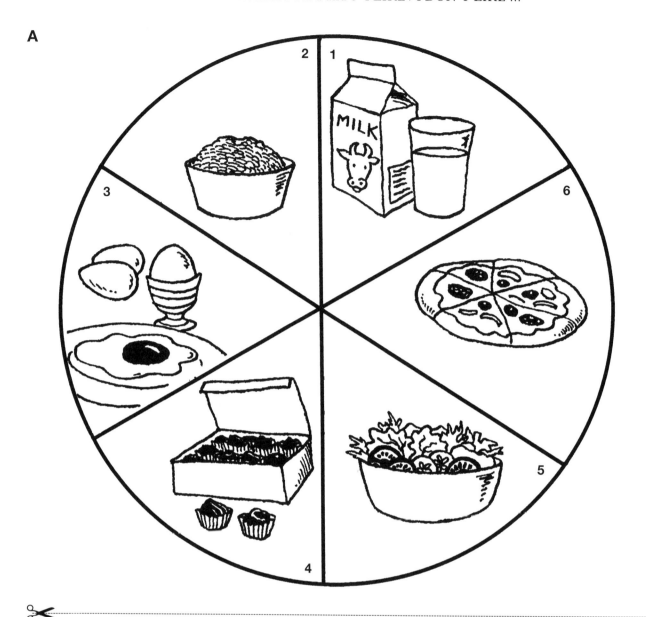

✂ -

B **Name** _____ **Class** _____ **Date** _____

I _____ milk.

I _____ pizza.

I _____ rice.

I _____ salad.

I _____ chocolates.

I _____ eggs.

This is Mark's family

This is Judy's family

Name _____ **Class** _____ **Date** _____

A: Which sentences go together? Draw a line to match them.

They are my friends.   She is happy.

Her hair is blond.   He is tall.

His hair is brown.   Their eyes are brown

B: Copy the sentences under the right picture.

Name _____ **Class** _____ **Date** _____

Day	Week 1	Week 2	Week 3	Week 4
Something that made me happy this week				

Name _____	Class _____	Date _____	
I like:	☺	😐	☹
learning English	☺	😐	☹
my books	☺	😐	☹
watching videos	☺	😐	☹
listening to cassettes	☺	😐	☹
singing songs	☺	😐	☹
role play	☺	😐	☹
playing games	☺	😐	☹
learning about other people	☺	😐	☹
reading stories	☺	😐	☹
	☺	😐	☹
	☺	😐	☹
	☺	😐	☹
	☺	😐	☹
	☺	😐	☹
	☺	😐	☹

WORKSHEET 8.3b OBJECTS FOR THE PICTURE OF ACHIEVEMENT

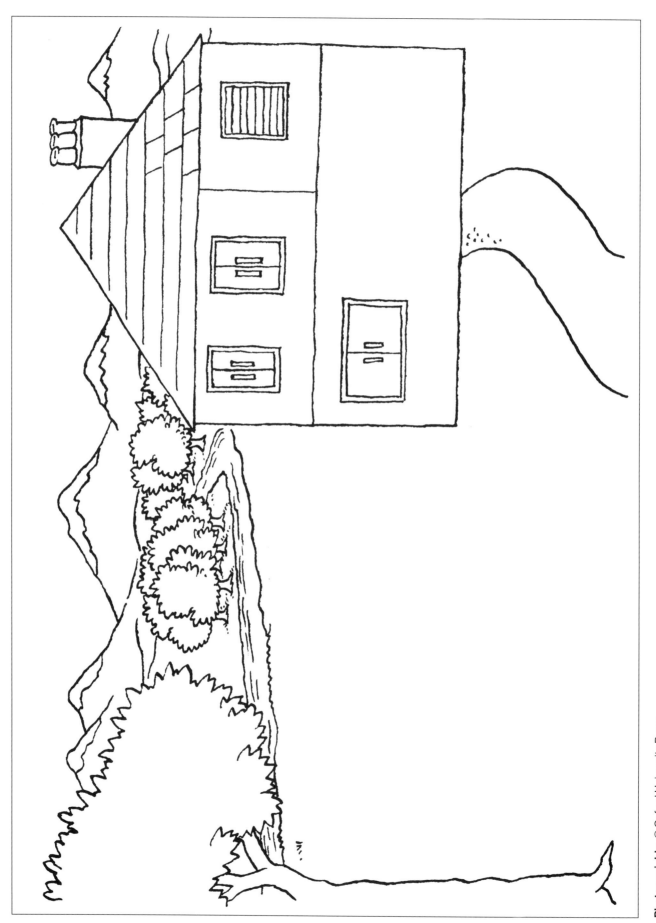

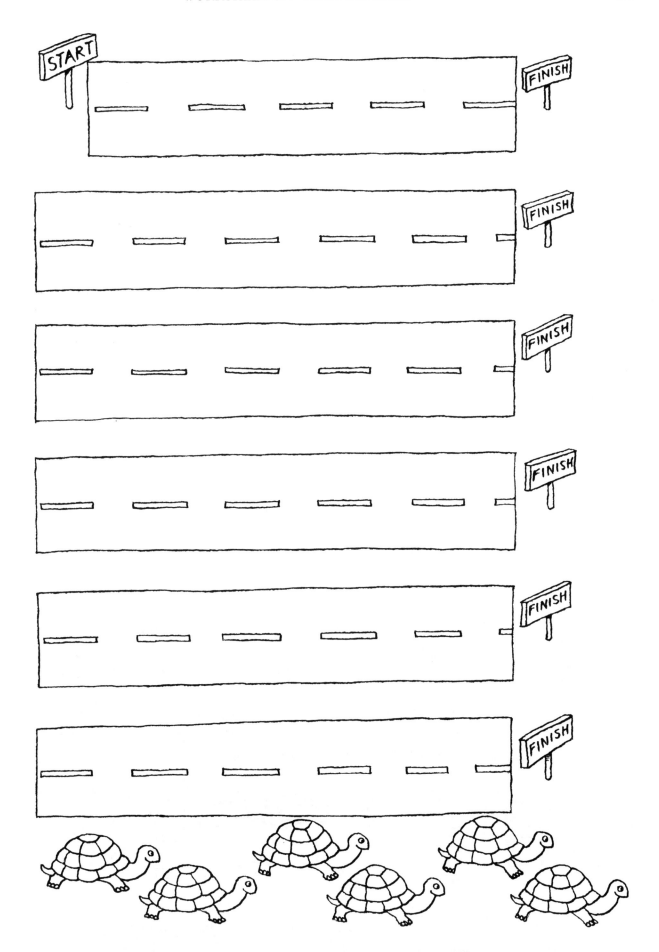

Name _____ **Class** _____ **Date** _____

Tick (✔) or circle the right picture.

1
  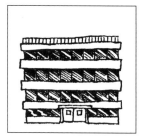 

Maria lives in a **bungalow** in a little village.

2

John loves **ice-skating** in winter.

3

When John's dog is very sick, he takes it to the **vet**.

4

Kate's birthday party is great! There's a **magician** playing with the children.

5

Peter drives carefully. He can't see very well because it's a **foggy** day.

Name _____ **Class** _____ **Date** _____

Part A

1 The story is called **The princess and the dragon**. Circle five words you think you will hear when you listen to the story.

fire   palace   king

prince   book   zoo

school   beautiful

Part B

Name _____ **Class** _____ **Date** _____

2 What do you think will happen now? Choose one answer.

1 The king is going to change his mind. ☐

2 The princess is going to run away. ☐

3 The dragon is going to fall in love with the princess. ☐

4 The dragon is going to get sick. ☐

Part C

Name _____ **Class** _____ **Date** _____

3 What do you think will happen next? Choose one answer.

1 The princess is going to get sick. ☐

2 A prince is going to come and save the princess. ☐

3 A good fairy is going to help the princess. ☐

4 The dragon is going to help the princess. ☐

Name _____ **Term/Semester** _____ **Class** _____

Date _____ **Absences** _____

Attitudes	
Homework	
Listening	
Speaking	
Reading	
Writing	

Other comments/suggestions	Overall grade

Student's comments

Parent's comments

Teacher's signature _____ Parent's signature _____

Name _____ **Term/Semester** _____ **Class** _____

Date _____ **Absences** _____

	Very good	Good	Satisfactory	Try harder	Comments
Listening	☐	☐	☐	☐	
Speaking	☐	☐	☐	☐	
Reading	☐	☐	☐	☐	
Writing	☐	☐	☐	☐	
Interest	☐	☐	☐	☐	
Effort	☐	☐	☐	☐	
Co-operation	☐	☐	☐	☐	
Class participation	☐	☐	☐	☐	
Homework	☐	☐	☐	☐	
Presentation of work	☐	☐	☐	☐	

Overall comments

Student's comments

Parents' comments

Teacher's signature _____ Parent's signature _____

	Name															
Attitudes towards learning English																
Shows interest in learning English.																
Tries hard.																
Co-operates well with classmates.																
Does homework regularly.																
Actively participates in classroom activities.																
Shows interest in target language culture(s).																
Listening																
Understands the main idea of a short spoken text.																
Recognizes reduced forms of words (e.g. has not = hasn't).																
Finds specific information from a short spoken text.																
Comprehends speech with unknown language when assisted by visual aids.																
Follows oral instructions.																
Speaking																
Gives personal information.																
Asks simple questions.																
Initiates communication.																
Participates in new situations, even with slight hesitation.																
Uses acceptable pronunciation and intonation.																
Uses most of vocabulary taught.																
Participates in oral pair and group work.																
Applies taught rules of grammar but may make some mistakes.																
Communicates without long pauses.																
Reading																
Reads sentences on his/her own.																
Recognizes punctuation symbols.																
Uses pictures to aid comprehension of new words.																
Begins to read silently.																
Comprehends the main idea of a short written paragraph.																
Comprehends the meaning of words relying solely on text.																
Understands detailed information stated explicitly in a short paragraph.																
Writing																
Has easily legible handwriting.																
Writes at an acceptable pace.																
Writes recognizable words even though sometimes slightly misspelled.																
Writes sentences using the basic English word order.																
Uses the vocabulary most frequently used in class.																
Writes a short paragraph based on a model.																
Usually spells core vocabulary correctly.																
Learning skills																
Keeps textbooks clean and tidy.																
Keeps exercise book tidy.																
Uses a picture dictionary.																
Keeps a tidy and regularly updated portfolio.																
Can evaluate own progress.																

I can _____ English

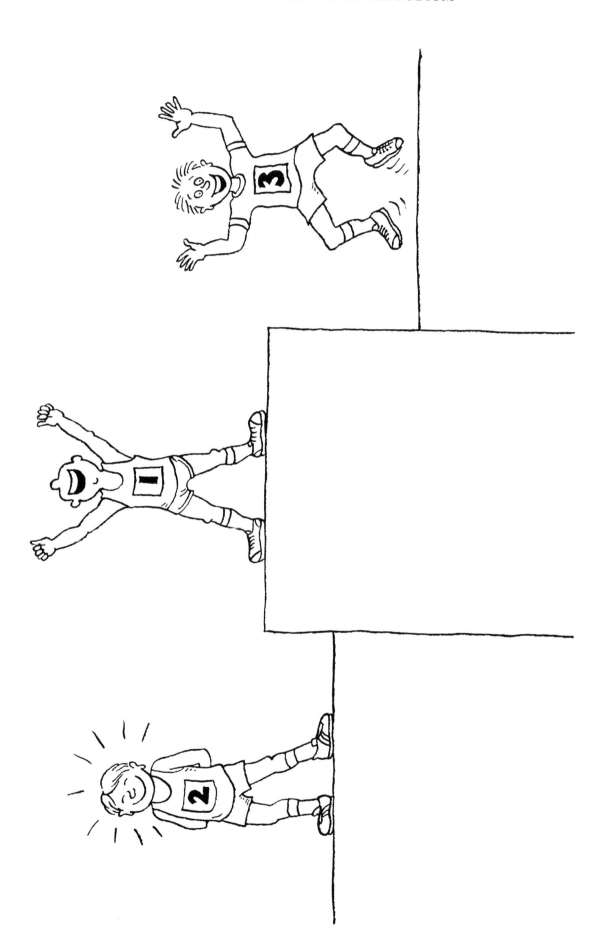

Name _____ **Class** _____ **Date** _____ **Absences** _____

	☺	😐	☹
Attitude and effort			
Likes learning about life in other countries.	☺	😐	☹
Likes working in pairs.	☺	😐	☹
Always does his/her homework.	☺	😐	☹
Listens to the teacher.	☺	😐	☹
Listening			
Can recognize the colours.	☺	😐	☹
Can recognize the numbers 1–10.	☺	😐	☹
Can recognize things he/she uses at school.	☺	😐	☹
Can understand a short dialogue on tape.	☺	😐	☹
Speaking			
Can introduce himself/herself.	☺	😐	☹
Can ask someone's name.	☺	😐	☹
Can count from 1–10.	☺	😐	☹
Can say the colours.	☺	😐	☹
Can say the names of things he/she uses at school.	☺	😐	☹
Can say the chants in the book.	☺	😐	☹
Reading			
Can recognize the colours.	☺	😐	☹
Can recognize the numbers from 1–10.	☺	😐	☹
Can recognize he things he/she uses at school.	☺	😐	☹
Writing			
Can copy words.	☺	😐	☹
Can write his/her name.	☺	😐	☹
Can write the numbers.	☺	😐	☹
Can write the colours.	☺	😐	☹

Student's comments:

Class _____ **Year** _____ **Date** _____

Attitudes											
Shows interest in other cultures.											
Shows interest in and enjoys the lessons.											
Pays attention in class.											
Does homework.											
Shows initiative.											
Shows willingness to help classmates.											
Shows respect and is friendly to his/her classmates.											
Learning and communication skills											
Keeps textbooks clean and tidy.											
Keeps exercise books tidy.											
Shows willingness to make guesses.											
Tries harder when encounters difficulties.											
Uses communication strategies and gestures to enhance his/her communicative ability.											
Asks for help from teacher and/or classmates when facing difficulties.											
Listening											
Understands spoken text even if it includes a few unknown words and structures.											
Understands the main idea of a short spoken text.											
Speaking											
Speaks with acceptable pronunciation and intonation.											
Volunteers contributions to class.											
Initiates communication with teacher/classmates.											
Speaks with acceptable accuracy.											
Participates in pair and group work.											
Reading											
Reads at an acceptable pace.											
Understands the main idea of a reading passage.											
Guesses meaning from context.											
Writing											
Writes with easily legible handwriting.											
Writes at an acceptable pace.											
Writes with acceptable accuracy (spelling, structures).											

Name _____ **Date** _____ **Class** _____ **Task** _____

Focus	Level	✓	Comments
Fluency	Frequent and long pauses cause difficulties in communicating.		
	Communicates even though there are some long pauses.		
	Communicates effectively without long pauses.		
Task achievement	Had difficulties in carrying out the task.		
	Carried out the task but with some difficulty.		
	Carried out the task successfully and with relative ease.		
Pronunciation	Pronunciation makes comprehension difficult.		
	Acceptable easily comprehensible pronunciation.		
	Very good pronunciation.		

Overall comments

Action suggested

Teacher's signature

Name _____ **Date** _____ **Class** _____ **Task** _____

Focus	Level	✓	Comments
Fluency	Frequent and long pauses cause difficulties in communicating.		
	Communicates even though there are some long pauses.		
	Communicates effectively without long pauses.		
Task achievement	Had difficulties in carrying out the task.		
	Carried out the task but with some difficulty.		
	Carried out the task successfully and with relative ease.		
Pronunciation	Pronunciation and/or inaccurate intonation makes comprehension difficult.		
	Acceptable, easily comprehensible pronunciation and intonation.		
	Very good pronunciation and intonation.		
Appropriateness	Difficulties in recognizing the degree of formality and/or in using appropriate language.		
	Recognizes the degree of formality but doesn't use appropriate language consistently throughout the task.		
	Recognizes degree of formality and uses appropriate language.		
Discourse management	Difficulties in initiating interaction and in responding.		
	Occasionally initiates interaction and responds promptly.		
	Initiates interaction and responds promptly.		

Overall comments

Action suggested

1

2

Teacher's signature

Name _____ **Date** _____ **Class** _____ **Task** _____

Focus	Level		Comments
Accuracy	Frequent grammatical mistakes cause difficulties in communicating.		
	Communicates even though there are some grammatical mistakes.		
	Communicates effectively without many grammatical mistakes.		
Task achievement	Had difficulties in carrying out the task.		
	Carried out the task but with some difficulty.		
	Carried out the task successfully and with relative ease.		
Handwriting	Handwriting makes comprehension difficult.		
	Acceptable easily legible handwriting.		
	Very legible handwriting.		
Mechanics (punctuation, capitalization, word boundaries)	Problems with mechanics make comprehension difficult.		
	Fair control of mechanics.		
	Very good control of mechanics.		

Overall comments

Action suggested

1

2

Teacher's signature

Further reading

See the Resource Books for Teachers website
http://www.oup.com/elt/teacher/rbt
for more activities and downloadable worksheets.

Baxter, A. 1997. *Evaluating Your Students.* London: Richmond.

Brumfit, C., J. Moon, and R. Tongue (eds). 1984. *Teaching English to Children: From Practice to Principle.* London: Nelson.

Cameron, L. 2001. *Teaching Languages to Young Learners.* Cambridge: Cambridge University Press.

Conner, C. 1998. *Assessment in Action in the Primary School.* London: Falmer Press.

Driscoll, P. and D. Frost. 1999. *The Teaching of Modern Foreign Languages in the Primary School.* London: Routledge

Genesee, F. and J. Upshur. 1996. *Classroom-based Evaluation in Second Language Education.* Cambridge: Cambridge University Press.

Halliwell, S. 1992. *Teaching English in the Primary Classroom.* Harlow: Longman.

Lowe, R. and F. Target. 1998. *Helping Students to Learn.* London: Richmond.

Moon, J. and M. Nikolov. (eds). 2000. *Research into Teaching English to Young Learners.* Pécs: Pécs University Press.

O'Malley, M. J. and L. Valdez-Pierce. 1996. *Authentic Assessment for English Language Learners.* Boston: Addison-Wesley.

Phillips, S. 1993. *Young Learners.* Oxford: Oxford University Press.

Phillips, D., S. Burwood, and H. Dunford. 1993. *Projects with Young Learners.* Oxford: Oxford University Press.

Rixon, S. (ed.) 1999. *Young Learners of English: Some Research Perspectives.* Harlow: Longman.

Grace, C., E. F. Shores, and K. Charner. 1998. *The Portfolio Book.* Beltsville, MD: Gryphon House.

Smith, K. 1997. 'Assessing and Testing Young Learners: Can we? Should we?' in *Entry Points: Papers from a Symposium of the Research, Testing and Young Learners Special Interest Groups.* Whitstable: IATEFL.

Vale, D. and A. Feunteun. 1995. *Teaching Children English.* Cambridge: Cambridge University Press.

Weir, C. 1993. *Understanding and Developing Language Tests.* Prentice Hall.

Index

General Index: references are to page numbers

Topics and Vocabulary Development: References are to activity numbers

Language Structures: References are to activity numbers

Other titles in the Resource Books for Teachers series

Primary Resource Books